# Table of Contents

| | |
|---|---|
| Dedication | 1 |
| With Special Gratitude | 3 |
| Foreword | 4 |
| Introduction | 5 |
| What Goes Up… | 8 |
| All or Nothing | 16 |
| Stepping Out on Faith | 34 |
| Up Against the Wall | 41 |
| Game Time | 52 |
| Faithful is the Lord | 66 |
| A New Direction | 74 |
| A Road to Remember | 85 |
| The Root | 98 |
| About the Author | 112 |

About-Face                                              Dimitri Rayner

# About-Face

## One Man's Journey from the Streets to Salvation

### Dimitri Rayner

Dimitri Rayner Ministries
Louisburg, North Carolina

Copyright © 2018 by Dimitri Rayner
All Right Reserved.
Printed in the United States of America

Published by Dimitri Rayner Ministries
Louisburg, North Carolina

ISBN: 978-1-7327743-0-8

No part of this publication may be reproduced, distributed or transmitted in any form or by any means, including photocopying, recording or other electronic or mechanical methods, without the prior written permission of the publisher, except with brief quotations embodied in critical reviews and certain other noncommercial uses permitted by copyright law. Request for permission should be emailed to dimitriraynerministries@gmail.com

Scriptures marked KJV are taken from the KING JAMES VERSION (KJV): KING JAMES VERSION, public domain.

Scripture taken from the New King James Version®. Copyright © 1982 by Thomas Nelson. Used by permission. All rights reserved.

Scriptures marked NLT are taken from the HOLY BIBLE, NEW LIVING TRANSLATION (NLT): Scriptures taken from the HOLY BIBLE, NEW LIVING TRANSLATION, Copyright© 1996, 2004, 2007 by Tyndale House Foundation. Used by permission of Tyndale House Publishers, Inc., Carol Stream, Illinois 60188. All rights reserved. Used by permission.

Scriptures marked NIV are taken from the NEW INTERNATIONAL VERSION (NIV): Scripture taken from THE HOLY BIBLE, NEW INTERNATIONAL VERSION ®. Copyright© 1973, 1978, 1984, 2011 by Biblica, Inc.TM. Used by permission of Zondervan

Scriptures marked NKJV are taken from the NEW KING JAMES VERSION (NKJV): Scripture taken from the NEW KING JAMES VERSION®. Copyright© 1982 by Thomas Nelson, Inc. Used by permission. All rights reserved.

Scriptures marked RSV are taken from the REVISED STANDARD VERSION (RSV): Scripture taken from the REVISED STANDARD VERSION, Grand Rapids: Zondervan, 1971.

Scriptures marked TLB are taken from THE LIVING BIBLE (TLB): Scripture taken from THE LIVING BIBLE copyright© 1971. Used by permission of Tyndale House Publishers, Inc., Carol Stream, Illinois 60188. All rights reserved.

Scriptures marked TM are taken from THE MESSAGE: THE BIBLE IN CONTEMPORARY ENGLISH (TM): Scripture taken from THE MESSAGE: THE BIBLE IN CONTEMPORARY ENGLISH, copyright©1993, 1994, 1995, 1996, 2000, 2001, 2002. Used by permission of NavPress Publishing Group

Cover Art by Ken Bledsoe, Moments and Memories

To order additional copies of this resource, visit www.DimitriRayner.com.

Connect with Dimitri on Social Media:
www.facebook.com/Dimitri-Rayner-2041143246158192/

To: Mrs Tina Peck

May the waters of God spring up & bring life to everything around you & in you.

*Dimitri Rayman*

# Dedication

Dedicated to my mother, Lillian Rayner, for pushing me to write this story. You loved me no matter what I did in life and I am so grateful you never turned your back on me, ever. I know you have God in you because you didn't just tell me about Him, your life displayed His character. It's because of you that I knew to call on the name of Jesus in my time of trouble, and that is worth more than any amount of money you could save up to give me as an inheritance. What you instilled in me as a child came alive when I surrendered to the Lord in adulthood. I love you Ma and hope who I am becoming makes you proud. You are the best and can never be replaced! May God bless you with all the desires of your heart because you are so deserving of God's best!

About-Face                                                Dimitri Rayner

# With Special Gratitude

I first want to thank my Lord and Savior, Jesus Christ, for without Him none of this would even be possible! Lord, you are the greatest gift to life, because without You, there is no life!

To the smile in my heart and my best friend. Valerie, you are the best wife ever. You rock with me and I am blessed beyond measure to have you as my First Lady!

To my daughter, my little princess Triniti. I love you and am honored to be your daddy.

To my daughters Adara and Ayanna. I love you like my very own.

To my Pastors and Spiritual parents, Apostle Dr. Shirley R. Brown and Mr. Fred Brown, you have indeed paved the way for me and are instrumental in my steps!

To my mentors Pastors Chris and Sherron Jordan. You've encouraged me since day one! Thank you for everything!

To my Destiny family, I love you all and I wouldn't want to be anywhere else!

To my big sister, Eionshafae Coppedge - Pope, who thought she was my momma growing up and still hasn't changed.

To Mr. and Mrs. Michael Brown, you were there for me in a very dark period of life and treated me as if I was one of your own. You will always be in my heart. I thank you and love you immensely!

To all the many other family and friends that play a part, thank you!

# Foreword

It is an honor and a privilege to write the foreword of a powerful real-life story with no fillers. The definition for About-Face is the reversal of attitude, behavior, or point of view and that is what you are about to encounter. ***"About-Face"*** is the book with a personal testimony of hope for the desperate. It is truly a turnaround story in real life. As you read, you will come into the author's life and feel the desperation for truth. The author shares his story not a status quo stereotyped young man, but a lost young man. The drug dealer turned to be the user and led his down spiraling until he is found in his processing chamber – the prison walls. Where he found out who he really was. He gave it all to God. This is not just another story about a drug dealer turning to Christ. This is the story about a heart change that enabled him to stay with Christ and win souls. The process of ***About-Face***.

Sit back and enjoy this work of truth. With great pleasure, I highly recommend this book to all - young, old, parents, children there is hope for all.

I also know the author personally and has had the privilege to work with him directly. He is my spiritual son, and I have spent time with him as he has patiently prepared himself with study, and faithful service to the ministry. He has been processed for this season in his life. Please enjoy Pastor Dimitri's moments of truth.


Thank you,

Dr. Shirley R Brown, Sr. Pastor
Destiny International Ministries, Raleigh, NC

# Introduction

Before I submitted my life to Jesus Christ and declared him as my personal Lord and Savior, my belief system on trust was all backwards. One of the hardest things to do is to convince someone to believe in something he cannot see, unless you say to them, "next Wednesday it is going to be 82 degrees." Now they'll believe that if you say the weatherman said it. But it's more difficult to get someone to believe in God who created the heavens and the earth and everything in it including the weather. To ask someone to trust God, you must first get them beyond the part of just believing in God, then work on the trust piece.

> **In the beginning God created the heavens and the earth.** *(Genesis 1:1)*

If someone would have asked me if I trust in Jesus Christ as Lord, I probably would have said, I believe He died on the cross and rose on the third day; meaning I believe He exists. As far as trust, I believed the word "trust" was a financial term of security which described how much money a person could access. If you possessed money, you were considered in good standing with people and they would trust you as someone who could meet their needs. But if you were broke, you would not be trusted as much, because you could not provide needed results. At this point of my life, I didn't comprehend that life changing results came from trusting in someone with more power than money or gold.

> **So be truly glad! There is wonderful joy ahead, even though the going is rough for a while down here. These trials are only to test your faith, to see whether or not it is strong and pure. It is being tested as fire tests gold and purifies it—and your faith is far more precious to God than mere gold; so if your faith remains strong**

after being tried in the test tube of fiery trials, it will bring you much praise and glory and honor on the day of His return. You love Him even though you have never seen Him; though not seeing Him, you trust Him; and even now you are happy with the inexpressible joy that comes from heaven itself. And your further reward for trusting Him will be the salvation of your souls. *(1 Peter 1:6-9, The Living Bible)*

As I live my life, I've learned something very profound. I've discovered that God has a plan for me just as He does for all who believe in Him.

**"For I know the plans I have for you," declares the Lord, "plans to prosper you and not to harm you, plans to give you hope and a future. Then you will call on me and come and pray to me, and I will listen to you. You will seek me and find me when you seek me with all your heart."** *(Jeremiah 29:11-13, New International Version)*

By God's grace and mercy something happened in my life, something BIG!!! My eyes were opened to a new reality on trust. In darkness I saw the light, a blue light that is! After this, my life would never be the same.

A time span of eight months of my life was parenthesized. A parenthesis is a comment or explanation of something in the narrative. The reason I say the eight months was parenthesized is because this part of my life was amplified! In mathematics parenthesis must be used when the procedures do not follow the normal order of operations. Even though it appeared my life was normal for my lifestyle, it was this time not going to follow the normal order of operation. A new formula was added to my life's equation.

Inside this parenthesis, I received the salvation of Jesus Christ. I learned how to have faith in God and He proved to me why I should put all my trust in

Him. I repeat God proved to me…! He showed me just how much He really loves me.

An about-face is a military command and means to turn around. It's a U-turn or a reversal. My life's direction at the time had to be retracted because I was headed towards self-destruction.

The bible says, Jesus took a few fish and loaves of bread and on different occasions fed multitudes of people by the thousands. I pray the contents of this book will be kind of just like a fish sandwich that feeds you and gives you a taste of God's goodness.

Bon appétit and welcome to the parenthesis that caused my U-turn away from destruction.

# What Goes Up…

What a cookout! I've been to a lot of cookouts in my life and as far as the selection of food, this one was one of the greats. It was not just burgers and hotdogs being served, but my homey was throwing steaks, leg quarters, ribs and even shrimp on the grill. There were tables set up with a wide variety of side dishes displayed to compliment all the delicious meats. Macaroni and cheese with a succulent melted cheese blend, potato salad, tossed salad, and pasta salad with beautiful red tomatoes and crisp cucumbers. They even served baked beans with meat. This is just to name a few but there was so much more to indulge in.

What a beautiful spring night this was. The cookout was really laid back and inviting. There were no more than 30 people in attendance and the music was a mixture of hip hop and R&B. The music was not that loud because we were in a neighborhood with a homeowner association but it was loud enough that all could party and enjoy themselves.

Beer and liquor was everywhere! And the best part was it's all free!!! All you had to do was be friends of the house, maybe drop a six pack in the cooler to show your appreciation and you had free reign on everything.

Homies were present and the ladies were all around. They were laughing and drinking and just having a good time. No one was acting stuck up or too good to talk to others. The ladies weren't dressed too provocative but just enough for the imagination to run wild especially after having a few drinks in your system. If you didn't make yourself known to be coupled up with someone, you could have easily been in the middle of some flirtatious activity that could have continued even after the cookout!

I did not come alone as I had three girls with me. I came with my girlfriend and her friend who were really looking forward to being in a different atmosphere on a Saturday night. We normally hung out at sports bars so this was going to be a real chill night for everyone.

The third girl I had with me was a dollar bill full of blow. Blow is powdered cocaine. When I wasn't high on blow, my days seemed dull and boring, but when I was high, everything in my mind seemed right. I was on top of the world, as if I was the main character in the movie classic "The Godfather," Don Corleone.

Even though I had fun partying all the time, I still always felt that there was something else missing. The money, the ladies and even the drugs never seemed to fill that empty void that was inside of me. I was desiring to be fulfilled but only focused on what I thought could achieve this. I heard God could fulfill all desires, needs and even wants but I didn't see Him attractive enough to really seek a relationship to give His fulfillment a chance.

I knew who God was because I grew up in the church. I got saved as a kid with my mother's suggestion and influence. Of course, she guided me through the process; however, even after that, growing up, my life was far from being on the highway to heaven. Later in life, I rededicated my life back to Jesus at the age of 29. Neither time did I take this confession serious enough to walk it out. The first time I was told to do it and the second time I did it out of my own emotions. I was not really committed to an about-face so my empty attempt didn't work out. I was going through a lot in life and it just seemed like the right thing to do.

I really had no concept of what being a Christian was all about, nor did I have a desire to find out. I lived by the motto "life is short" and I'm going to live my life the way I want. I would do this until I got tired and much older, and then, only then, I would get serious about God. It made sense to me to wait until I was ready to get settled. I knew heaven and hell were real and my belief was if I repented right before I died, I would make it into heaven. It may have been by the "skin of my teeth," but I would have got in. With no real concept of what being saved was all about, I didn't know Christianity was all about having a personal relationship with Jesus.

However, what I did know, without a shadow of a doubt, was how to have a good time and this cookout was it. It was so good that after partying Saturday night, I was willing to come back for a repeat on Sunday, even though I had to work the next day.

Sunday night wasn't as thick with people as Saturday, but all the same ingredients were there. I didn't need a crowd to get super tipsy nor high on blow. As a matter of fact, the fewer the people, the better, meaning more for me. I wasn't real hungry anyway so I could just get a "to go" plate. All I really wanted was the atmosphere.

All the warning signs were there telling me it was time to go home. My money was low, the gas in the jeep was low and just the fact that it was already after 10:00 p.m. and I had to go to work the next day. The incentive to stay longer was being enticed by the fact I still had "blow" in my bill and beer and liquor as a chaser. Seeing this was the situation at hand, the party wasn't over until all the goodies were gone. I did though have to take in to account that I stayed past my cutoff time and I promised my girl I wouldn't be out that late. I decided it was time for me to leave, so back home I headed.

The night breeze was perfect for a slow drive with the windows down and of course the music had to be loud. As I remember, I was listening to that 1998, AZ "Pieces of a Man" album. That was my style of hip-hop! That blow really had me in a zone and I could feel myself traveling back in time to when I considered my life to be good, those "Get Money Days!"

The past seemed to have a power over me that I could never seem to shake. With the good came a lot of bad, along with a lot of ugly when I was in the drug business. It was many times hard to focus on my future because of what I know now to have been a stronghold that was keeping me stuck in one place. Strongholds are faulty thinking patterns based on lies and deception. It's a weapon the devil uses to keep us from moving forward into the best that God has for us. A lot of people have strongholds in their lives and don't even realize it.

I believed deep in my heart, I would never be anywhere near the man I once was as a drug dealer, who had "so called" say so in this world. I thought my best days were in my past even though they were filled with hurt and pain and a whole lot of lies. I was still in a place of hurt and did not want to acknowledge all the wounds I was carrying inside me.

I had now become addicted to drugs and alcohol and could never really feel like someone powerful or meaningful unless I was high, reminiscing on the past. Whenever I was high, I could be whoever I wanted. I just didn't want to be me in my current condition. After the addictions piled on, I became very uncomfortable in my own skin.

One of my old homies said, if I ever got a million dollars in my hand, I would overdose. That statement bothered me; he was right. At that time of my life, I would have died from partying and never enjoyed the money.

I not only smoked weed and sniffed coke but I was a big undercover fan of wooly blunts. I say undercover because I tried to hide what I was doing although it began to show itself without me saying a word. Woolies are cigars laced with crack cocaine. They are often rolled with either weed or the cigar tobacco from the blunt depending on preference. Weed for me normally mellowed the cocaine, so I preferred the tobacco to give me a more intense high. No mellowing for me!

Another homeboy used to call me a cool junkie. I could dress real fresh, but would get so high on drugs at times that I would be "flying higher than a helicopter," so to speak.

I never knew how much Satan had deceived me until I came into the knowledge of Jesus Christ. Jesus Christ says:

**"Whoever commits sin is a slave of sin."** *(John 8:34)*

**An evil man is held captive by his own sins; they are ropes that catch and hold him.** *(Proverbs 5:22, New Living Translation)*

**And you shall know the truth, and the truth shall make you free.** *(John 8:32)*

Now before I learned the truth, my life's truth was, I loved to get high and party. If I could just get to my destination, this night would go down as one of the good ones. I was looking forward to finishing my dollar bill, drinking the rest of my beer and then calling it a night.

I finally made it back home and was relieved I didn't get stopped by the police. Now after driving from the other side of town, I realized I left my work clothes for the next day at my mother's house. I would have to again drive back to the other side of town to get them. Another fifteen minutes driving. I didn't really want to go back there especially since I was feeling so nice and in a zone. And on top of that, it was already late!

My mother is a Christian and just being who she is, I didn't want to disrespect her by showing up at her door step having to run in and run out at that time of night, but I was left with no choice.

Earlier that day my mother and I had a bad argument and it wasn't pretty. She told me the devil was about to set me up because I was still drinking and driving plus I had no driver's license. I was within two months of coming off probation from two prior DUIs and would have been eligible for a driver's license hearing with DMV within the next three months after that.

Drinking and driving always seem to trap me off which means to set me up for failure. Here I go again putting myself in the same situation out in the open water where the sharks are lurking. The open water is what I referred to as the streets and the sharks is what I called the police. Eventually my drinking and driving always get me the same results which is nowhere fast.

Remembering my mother fussing at me earlier that day had blown my buzz and I had to start all over again. I did not want a repeat tonight. I can honestly say I felt bad because my mother is a good woman and I know she only wanted the best for me. However, by my choice this was my way of life, so If I could just get there and get my work clothes with no arguments, I'll be good. I just want to get back to my girl's house with no problems.

My girl was not feeling me going back out and driving her jeep. "Hurry up and come back," she said, "and be careful!" I took another hit of that powder and was ready to make this quick turnaround trip. Music still cranking loud, I pulled off and a rush of confidence hit me. "I got this," I said! I looked both ways before exiting the apartment complex and noticed I was the only one on the road.

It was now about 11:30 p.m. and I was riding dirty with no driver's license. Riding dirty, meaning I had something illegal in my possession while driving. After I turned out, I drove down the road about a hundred yards then looked in the rear-view mirror and saw a police car was now right behind me. The police, like a shark in the water, snuck up behind me. This reminded me of the old classic movie "Jaws" where this killer shark always came out of nowhere and attacked! Where in the world did this cop come from? He must have dropped out of the sky; but I figured if I turned the music down and drove straight, he would just go around me. "No swerving" was my motto!

I made it to the red light and I am just praying this officer goes around me and bothers someone else. I am not the fish you want tonight. Just let me go about my business! The light turns green and then it happened, BLUE LIGHTS!

It started out with only one police car but then I looked and there was a second car. I've had my share of jumping out and running from the police, but that was when I was much younger and had more to lose because of the quantity of drugs I was carrying. I was now at the age of thirty-five, a few months from thirty-six and was not in a running mood. Honestly, it wasn't my age, it was the fact that I was just too high to run! The officer came to the window and said, "I pulled you over because after running the tag, I could see the owner's driver's license is suspended." The owner is a female so what are you stopping me for was the question I asked myself?

When I told the officer "I didn't have a driver's license", he flashed his light through the vehicle. I was drinking a beer when I was pulled so I had quickly rolled the beer under the passenger seat to stash it. As he is looking through the vehicle with the flashlight, to my dumb surprise the beer bottle rolled back down in open view.

I know what happens next because I have been down this road before, many other times. It's time for me to do what I do best and step out of the car. The officer did not believe the story I told him about someone being in the backseat and leaving the beer bottle without me knowing. Nor did he believe I had only consumed a couple of beers many hours earlier. To be honest I'd just had a swallow of the beer before he pulled behind me. If I had known this was going to happen, I would have at least finished the beer before I pulled off. Before they ask you to step out of the car, they call for backup and once backup arrives, the drunk man tests begin. I guess that was the reason for the second police car.

I didn't want to take those tests. All I wanted to do was drive away and go home. Before the officer ever came to the window, I sat in the jeep and prayed for mercy from a God I wasn't serving. I was hoping if I prayed hard enough, God would have looked out for me and allow the officer to let me go on to my destination. He had looked out for me so many other times before it wasn't even funny. It didn't work this time because here I go having to now step out of the vehicle.

My advantage, I knew how to handle my alcohol. And even though I failed sobriety tests four times in the past, tonight I was going to represent the non-licensed, drinking and drivers well. I thought I did pretty good except for that walking the straight-line part and having to spin around and then comeback.

Now here I am thinking I'm good to go and the most dreadful thing happened. This, I will never for the rest of my life forget. One of the officers after checking his computer said there was a warrant for my arrest, regarding a DWLR (driving while license revoked) and a no seat belt ticket that I failed to handle. I was on my way to jail regardless!

I knew this couldn't be true because I had a lawyer two years prior handling two DUIs I received within two weeks of each other. He was also handling a few other minor tickets and these were included in that stack. No matter how well I thought I did on the sobriety test that was all irrelevant at this point. Then come to find out, they were still charging me with a new DUI so obviously they didn't like the way I took the test or what I blew in the breathalyzer.

I was just thankful that out of all that searching those two cops did in that jeep, they never found my coke stash. I had put the rest of the blow folded up in a dollar bill in an empty cigarette pack and tucked it way down between the seats. I had just opened a fresh pack of Newport cigarettes and that was all they saw. All I can say is God was truly on my side. The warrant was bad and the new DUI was bad but to have gotten a possession of cocaine charge would have made it even worse and truly exposed me. It would have ruined everything. I am thankful that was still hidden and not found out.

So here I go again taking this ride. I've taken a few rides off to jail in my day so I was not new to this road trip. The only thing different now was I was tired of the familiar. I was finally sick and tired of being sick and tired. There is nothing cool about going to jail and of course not cool to continuously repeat the same thing over and over. What point was I trying to prove? How much I can screw up my own life? How much I can fail to comprehend life's learning lessons being shown to me? Same things get you same results and I was not immune.

That night I learned God shows mercy even to those who don't serve Him.

> **But God, who is rich in mercy, because of His great love with which He loved us, even when we were dead in trespasses.**
> *(Ephesians 2:4, 5a)*

# All or Nothing

I was never one to accept loss very well and found it difficult to conform to a losing lifestyle. I learned in the streets there was a right way to do wrong. Whenever I got caught up, I believed it was because I didn't do the wrong correctly or someone else screwed it up for me. I would always try to rework my plan for a better outcome which had to be to my benefit. A personal gain was what I desired whether I was dealing drugs, using drugs or whatever my scheme was at that time. I never really knew how selfish I was until those jail steel doors closed behind me.

I didn't have any money for bail and the magistrate said the state was going to auction off the vehicle I was driving. It didn't matter to them that the jeep belonged to someone else. The fact of me being the driver and a repeat offender was the only concern they had. You would have thought that after losing my own vehicle to the state three years prior, for the same reason, I would have learned my lesson. It's clear the lesson wasn't learned, and now this time, I jeopardized someone else's property. Worse than that, I was still drinking.

I remember making the call to my mother from the holding cell because I couldn't get through to my girl. She was very worried and trying to figure out how she could get me out of jail. I was no longer a drug dealer and my money was not like it used to be, plus I had expensive habits.

My main concern at the time was just for my girl to get her jeep back. I could have cared less about me and didn't feel she should suffer for my lack of responsibility. I also knew it was not my mother's responsibility to clean up my mess.

As much as I wanted to go home, jail was the best place for me at this point. I just wanted to "man up" for my actions and face whatever consequences I had coming.

**Whatever a man sows, that he will also reap.** *(Galatians 6:7)*

My entire body was numbed and all I could think about was my irresponsibility just affected someone very important to me. This was not the first time my actions had caused others pain but now I was really seeing all the pain and distress I had brought on to other people. I was hoping my girl still had my back and had forgiven me. She had to be worried about me and not being able to contact her was driving me crazy. Not hearing her voice was difficult to bear. I never knew how much the relationship meant to me until now.

There were a few others in the holding cell with me and I'm not sure which one of them it was but someone smelled like they hadn't had a bath in days. Someone kept fussing and mumbling and cussing out loud as if someone was paying attention to his request. If only I had not gone to this party, I would not be in this predicament.

It seemed like forever I was in this cell but it was only about four or five hours–a lifetime when you can't open the door and walk out on your own. The smell of urine was getting on my nerves and all I could think was "Dimitri, you did it again." I asked myself, "Dimitri, how could you!"

More than anything, I just wanted the pain to go away. My first court appearance made matters worse and confirmed what I felt inside regarding my release. I was not leaving anytime soon. My bond for the DWLR and no seat belt was a secured bond for $2,000. The DUI, was secured at $7,500. I couldn't afford either of these and didn't want anyone else to pay on my behalf.

I was ready and knew this was the beginning of a long journey. This numbness was indescribable and had taken over my entire body. I didn't want to talk to anyone at all about anything.

As crazy as it sounds, I was mainly concerned about my relationship status with my girlfriend and wondering where my life was headed.

I was yelling and screaming on the inside for help, but it seemed no one heard my cry. It felt like my death was near and I was exhausted. It was not just a physical death I was fearing but an internal death. I felt as if I was just passing away to nothing.

I didn't realize God heard every yell and scream happening on the inside of me. I could feel deep down in my soul this was my last chance at hope and at life. For me to live, the old me had to die.

I was soon taken to the dorm in jail where I would be held until my scheduled court dates. No bribery could have allowed me to walk out those gates. In the American court system, no bail money means no release until you go before the judge. The judge would pass sentence on failure to appear for driving while license revoked, no seat belt, a new DUI charge and a probation violation charge. I had one DUI in the state of Georgia and now four in North Carolina.

What in the world was I thinking? This lifestyle has got to come to an end. Just let me do what I must to get to where I have to be. The sooner I could do this with no disturbances, the sooner I could go home. I didn't want any new homies, I just wanted peace.

As I looked around the dorm, I noticed so many who seemed to be comfortable and enjoying themselves. This was not where I wanted to find comfort nor did I see any peace.

In this type of environment, there is a lot of time to think about everything. I began thinking about things I did years prior which played a major part in me being where I was physically, mentally and spiritually.

The most important part of me, is my spiritual life. My spiritual life seemed non-existent. I knew by name who Jesus Christ was and believed He existed. I even referenced Him on many occasions but just not as MY Lord and Savior. He was God; I just didn't participate in His way of life.

My soul's survival was in jeopardy because of my vain life choices. I had never hurt so much. I felt as if my life was being snatched from me and I was awoken to feel it. It was like the wind being knocked out of me yet I was still able to speak. Being in a place of deep hurt birthed unhappiness for me. I knew a long time ago of my depleted spiritual state but now had to face me, the man in the mirror.

It was only two days after my arrest and now the hurt and disgust of myself became so unbearable that I had to lie down on my bunk. I wasn't really feeling anything that was going on around me; I just pulled the covers up over my head. I wanted to disappear and be somewhere else away from everything. I felt trapped and needed out. I wanted this pain to go away. I began crying and called on Jesus for help.

    Something was happening inside of me. I tried to muffle the sound of my crying so as to not be heard and not make any noticeable shakes or movements. I didn't want to alert anyone of my tears because jail was not a place to show tears or weakness. And as tough as I was, I finally realized the weakness and helplessness of my current state. I needed help from someone much bigger than me.

    In the middle of my crying, I asked Jesus Christ to come into my heart and He did. I knew He existed but never knew Him personally. I may not have said a traditional "sinner's prayer" as some may call it, but I cried from my heart to Him and He responded immediately. It was as if He was waiting for me right there on that bunk, right under those covers.

    Although I was locked up facing charges that could have given me prison time, I didn't even care about all of that. I had just made the best life decision of all time. Not jail time nor prison time could take that away from me.

    I remembered my mother told me:

**For God so loved the world that He gave His only begotten Son, that whoever believes in Him should not perish but have everlasting life.** *(John 3:16)*

Even though I had given my life to Christ as a kid and went through the motions of rededicating my life back to God when I was older, this time was completely different.

    What made this time different from before? I wasn't pushed by anyone and no one had suggested it to me. I also wasn't moving out of emotions either. I wanted life and I could only get it through Jesus. I wanted Him and this time I wasn't going to allow anything to keep me from this personal relationship. I screwed up a lot of years of my life and now was time to take a different avenue.

> **The result was all gain, no loss. Distress that drives us to God does that. It turns us around. It gets us back in the way of salvation. We never regret that kind of pain. But those who let distress drive them away from God are full of regrets, end up on a deathbed full of regrets** *(2 Corinthians 7:9b-10, Message)*

I knew deep down I couldn't go back out on the streets the same way I left. I was miserable and wanted all the habits and choices that kept me from having a better life to just go away. In my weeping prayer, I asked God to take the taste of alcohol and drugs from me. These two strongholds held me down long enough and it was now time for them both to depart. I needed God to give them their walking papers.

I've tried in the past but they always made their way back home to me. It was as if they had a room in my house or drawer in my closet. I would kick them out, but they would always return as if they had a door key or their name was on the lease, so they never left.

I now had a confidence in knowing if I asked God to kick them out He would be able to do it successfully. I didn't know how, but just knew He could. I went to God in desperation because I could not fix my life.

I heard a voice so clearly speak to me and I knew it was God. It was not an audible voice but I still heard it. It seemed like it was out loud under the covers with me. The voice asked me, "What about cigarettes?" Now I've tried quitting before but it was only for a short time. I figured if He took away the alcohol and drugs I would be good because that was the problem in my life. I didn't think cigarettes caused an issue. They were almost normal. I then heard God say, "All or nothing." The reason the cigarettes had to go was because they were the gateway to my other addictions. When I smoked most of the time a drink was not far from my mind, neither was anything else. "All or nothing" was proposed to me and it didn't take me long to accept what He offered. Even though I had a choice, I didn't! I was in a place I had never been before with God and a moment I will never forget. I told God it would be "All."

From this moment on my life would never be the same, it was clear. The very God I ignored and hadn't acknowledged came when I got in a desperate place and I knew to call on Him. Jesus met me right in jail. I believe with all my heart that He was waiting for me.

**No one can come to Me unless the Father who sent Me draws him.** *(John 6:44)*

I pray my heavenly Father will draw you closer to my Lord Jesus today. Ask Him and He will do it for you. Ask and you shall receive! It doesn't matter what you have gone through or what you have done. He will draw you close to Him, right in His arms if you want to be there.

The next morning, I had this strong craving for a bible. I looked where the books in the dorm were kept and not a bible in sight. I had to wait until one was returned but day after day, no bible. Finally, a guy in a bunk near me was leaving and I asked him if I could have his bible and he said yes. It was a pocket-sized Gideon's bible that was the New Testament only with Psalms and Proverbs included. I was so excited to get this bible as if I'd struck gold. This truly was much better than gold and more profitable than hitting the lottery. Money can't buy revelation of God's Word nor can it produce the divine instructions for my life's plan. My pathway was in the bible. It was my new road map. I had to read to learn and so my journey in the Word of God began.

A guy I was locked up with showed me how I could order a new study bible through the county. This bible was also a New Testament only but it was setup for new believers like myself. It had so many study topics and I was eager to begin reading. Once I received it, I read the entire New Testament, all but the last book of the bible called Revelation. I knew the book of Revelation was going to take some time and understanding and I didn't know if it would make sense to me. I just wanted to learn as much as I could about Jesus and where I fit in this new life as a Christian. I was curious about my purpose and what I was to do next.

I didn't know much about the Holy Spirit and how He operated. I just knew there was a connection. A guy in the dorm walked up to me and said the Holy Spirit told him to let me read a book he had called, "Battlefield of the Mind," by Joyce Meyer. I didn't know who Joyce Meyer was, but I was interested in what this book had to say.

> "Our past may explain why we're suffering but we must not use it as an excuse to stay in bondage." (Joyce Meyer, "Battlefield of the Mind: Winning the Battle in Your Mind")

The Lord must of really knew I still needed help, because even though I gave my life to Christ, I was still hurting. I hadn't talked to my girl nor had I received a letter from her. Immediately, I started the book and read it in three days. The Battlefield book was encouraging and I learned a lot. I just needed to apply what I read. I also read it so fast that I'm sure I missed a lot of key instructions. I did however remember that changing my mind was changing my life. I just had to learn how to begin to think like God. Now that is the real challenge!

I also began reading books by Smith Wigglesworth on faith. His faith was that he believed God to perform creative miracles in all areas of our lives no matter what it looked like. That was some real kind of faith that I needed to change my way of thinking about myself and about how I viewed God!

> "There is nothing impossible with God. All the impossibility is with us when we measure God by the limitations of our unbelief." (Smith Wigglesworth)

I needed all I could to give me a boost and to help me get through and endure. I was willing to do what it took to walk this walk out, but even in that, my mind would begin to wonder at times. Sometimes I would wonder what my girl was doing and with who.

The guy who gave me the books to read was also a Christian and he encouraged me a lot. I really needed that and glad God placed him in my life at that season. He encouraged me to pray about everything and everybody, basically all my interactions.

I wrote out a long list of things and people to pray about. I prayed for the judge, the DA, my attorneys and their families as well. If it came to mind I prayed about it. I even prayed about my relationship with my own family. I prayed my little girl would know her daddy loved her because she was only three years old when I left. I asked the Lord to whisper in her ear and let her know I loved her.

All this praying was so new to me. I was trying to do something different for different results.

My new brother in Christ kept encouraging me as I was down at times and trying to fight through this thing. I truly had a battle going on in my mind and had a long process ahead of me to go through before it would get any easier.

I kept trying to tell myself my girl was waiting for me. "I'm not worried, I'm good." The days at times seemed to go by slow and seemed to get longer and longer. But still no letter from her.

The good thing in all of this was I was getting closer to my court date. This faith thing had me going and Proverbs 3:5-6 became my favorite scripture.

> **Trust in the Lord with all your heart, and lean not on your own understanding; In all your ways acknowledge Him, and He shall direct your paths.** *(Proverbs 3:5-6)*

I was now learning how to trust God and rely on Him. This was one of the hardest things I've ever done. When you are used to doing things one way for so long, it's hard and a real challenge to do them differently. To wait on God and His timing was not easy. In all of this, God knew what I needed and when I needed it. I was being stripped of my old self but didn't realize it. Slowly but surely a transformation was taking place. The old me was dying.

Every time I called home, I was being told by my mother to focus on God only and things would get better. Other people who were praying for me relayed the same message to her to give to me. Okay, that is easier said than done, however, I will try. Praying and reading the Word of God is what got me through some of the toughest days and nights of my life. I was in so much emotional pain, but God has a way of comforting that is unexplainable. I am so blessed that God even placed people in my life to encourage me in His Word. I also had to come to a place of encouraging others in the Word, even while I was going through my own painful transformation.

It was a push to help the next man especially when I was battling myself. I didn't always feel like telling others to stay focused. I didn't feel like even talking to anyone either. Sometimes I just wanted to be to myself wrapped up in my own feelings of loneliness and deep thought. I mean who was I to encourage somebody when I myself wanted a shoulder to cry on at times. It was a struggle true indeed yet I still encouraged anyone I could. Truth is, nothing is greater than the Lord and He does the impossible easily. He takes those weak moments and provide His strength. That is what made things easier for me to get through day to day. It was not my own strength but His!

I decided I would write my girl and wait for a response. I was hoping she just didn't know how to write me and was waiting for a letter from me. In this letter, I would express all my feeling towards her. This was something I had never really done before. I'm a new man and have a new attitude about life. Because I was going to court the following month in June, I prayed to get a quick return letter back from her.

I really believed I was going home because my faith in God had gone to a new level. I had never put faith in God to work before. On prior offenses, I put my faith in the attorneys that I paid; believing they would do their part and get an outcome that would be in my favor. I didn't know, that even God, played a major part in that as well. This time was very different because I had no money. I had a court appointed attorney, who I've so far had only seen once, and I never knew what my case was looking like. The Lord had been working in my favor all these other times before just to give me a wake-up call. He loves me so much that He repeatedly gave me chance after chance! However, I never acknowledged Him. This time God made sure I was in a place to *only* acknowledge Him. What I was going through, *only* He could help me and *only* He could deliver me.

My prayers were finally answered. My girl had finally written me back. I didn't know what to expect in this letter so I was hesitant about even opening it. It's crazy how you can wait for something so long and when you finally get it, you pause. Well here goes nothing! She basically expressed her struggles, her pain and that she was trying not to blame me for all she was going through. She didn't want to talk to me right now because her life was completely upside down. She wasn't happy about not having her jeep as this was her only means of transportation. She was a working woman with a child and transportation was vital. She worked hard to purchase her jeep so why should she have to suffer for my irresponsibility.

I knew I had messed up bad; this was not what I wanted to hear. I really wanted to make things better for her financially, but all I could do was pray. I asked the Lord to forgive me for what I had done to cause her frustration. I also prayed she would forgive me as well.

It was crazy because all these women I had run game on, all the times I cheated on women, even on her, now I was trying to be committed. It had to be God because, if I was still on the streets, I'd be doing what I was doing before, which was being with whoever I wanted to. I had to ask myself was I really in love or just lonely!

I did love her, I just didn't know how to love properly and it reflected in my actions.

During my time of preparing to go to court, I began to fast. This was my first time ever fasting. I fasted for thirteen and a half days straight. Nine of those days, I only ate my breakfast tray which was served about 4:45 a.m. each morning. I would give away my lunch and dinner tray to whomever I felt led to. After those nine days were up, I continued fasting four and a half more days, consuming no food and water at all.

I remember one guy in lockup, who was a Muslim, realized what I was doing and told my Christian brother I couldn't go three days without food and water and survive. After day four, the Muslim was very quiet yet astonished. While fasting, I learned more about God. I really saw He was a keeper and comforter in hard times. I was hungry and thirsty; yet, I was sustained.

I led some bible studies with a couple of the brothers. We had what you would call, "prayer calls," at the end of each night before the lights went out. It never happened unless someone yelled, "PRAYER CALL!" After prayer call was made, some guys would come together into a big circle and then the one leading the prayer call would begin praying until the end of the day before we all would go to sleep.

The guy who started leading the prayer calls ended up on some strong daily medication that would put him to sleep long before prayer calls were to be called. The first night the guy fell asleep early and someone said to me, "I sure missed prayer call tonight." The Lord then laid it on my heart to be the one to call it going forward. I felt funny and weird about it because I felt like I was bringing attention to myself. Why me?

God showed me it was bringing attention to Him and not me. This was a part of me getting boldness and not being embarrassed when people would look at me in this manner. I was a child of God and not ashamed of it.

Sometimes in prayer call, I would just say the Lord's prayer and it would be amusing how another guy who was a Muslim, and known as being a "real tough guy" would join in the circle. This guy had a reputation in the jail as a "knockout artist" meaning he was known to knock peopled out in fights.

However, even as a Muslim, he would repeat the Lord's prayer when it was prayed. This really showed me that the Lord can touch anyone's heart and show Himself to whomever He wants. No one is exempt!

On my first court date, I was a little nervous yet remained calm. My brother said to me, "If the outcome is not what you hoped, do not come back in here looking sad. Walk in with your head high." Now deep down inside, I was in assurance, that today, I was going home.

I understood exactly what he meant. I never want to make it seem like Jesus couldn't deliver me and I show disappointment in Him. A bad reaction from me could hinder the message I was saying I believed. I loved my Lord and whether He does it or not, I know He can, and I am content with that. Jesus had my vote regardless!

My case was the last one to be heard on this day. The court appointed attorney I saw one time was not the attorney who showed up. This unknown attorney came out to me in the holding cell and said, "The original attorney thought I was more qualified to handle your case." In the middle of him telling me this, the bailiff came out and said, "The Judge is not wavering on the DUI charge." This alone carries a two-year sentence. The only thing the judge was willing to hear was the DWLR with no seat belt and the failure to appear charges. The attorney suggested I request a continuance or even fight it because of some legalities involving the traffic stop.

Something in me said no continuance and no need to argue because I was guilty. I just wanted to accept responsibility for my wrong doings and receive whatever punishment I was due even though my attorney was completely against my decision.

After entering the court room, I saw my mother and her dear friend. Her friend was like my mom's sister and very much family to me. Those two were praying in the spirit on my behalf. Praying in the spirit is using a language that we as believers of Jesus Christ have access to when receive the baptism of the Holy Spirit. This allows you to pray directly to the Heavenly Father in the name of Jesus and the devil cannot understand what you are saying therefore he cannot intercept. Their prayers were going straight to heaven on my behalf!

Something happened in that courtroom that is still unexplainable! My representing attorney told the judge, contrary to his advice, I, the client, wanted to proceed with the hearing. All I know is, I began to weep and couldn't stop. The judge said the charge carries a sentence of twenty-four months because of my history. The attorney told him I was a former Marine as part of the mitigating factors. A mitigating factor, in law, is any information or evidence presented to the court regarding the defendant or the circumstances of the crime that might result in reduced charges or a lesser sentence.

In the background, I was still weeping. The judge stated to me, that he needed a moment to rethink because the help I required was not on the outside. After a couple of minutes of looking over my paperwork, the judge came back and ruled on a four-month sentence. I didn't go home that day but was going home sooner than the original plan the judge had laid out for me.

The Lord showed me favor and at the time I couldn't explain all that happened and how the tables turned. Now I know it was due to repentance! I was truly sorry about what I'd done and I just couldn't stop weeping. I literally saw the judge have a change of heart. What he said he wouldn't do, he did it and that was because of God. He can touch anyone's heart that He wants.

There is no power like the power of God. Even as I am writing this, it still brings tears to my eyes because I literally saw God turn things around on my behalf. It was all for His glory because only Jesus could deliver me and He did. The devil no longer had anything to hold over my head because I confessed the truth out of my own mouth and it paid off.

**Now I know that the Lord saves His anointed; He will answer him from His holy heaven with the saving strength of His right hand.**
*(Psalm 20:6)*

The Lord was showing me why I should trust Him. No gold or any amount of money could have bought the experience that I had on that day in the courtroom. When leaving, the bailiff said to me, "In all my years of knowing this judge, he has never gone back and changed a sentence." Just hearing him say that confirmed what I saw with my own eyes that God intervened for me.

When I got back to the dorm, I remembered to keep my head up. Although I wasn't going home that day, there was still victory. I wanted one thing to happen but something better happened. I wanted to go home, and when told I was staying, I was at peace. My faith in God was beginning to show me how hearing Not Yet doesn't mean No!

Guys greeted me when I came back and asked what happened. I gave the verdict and said it's all good. If anything negative was said about me or God it wasn't said to me but I didn't care because I knew somehow, someway God had me and this was going to work out for my good.

The next day two young guys came in to the dorm. One was assigned to the bunk above me and the other to the top bunk right next to the other guy. The young guy above had a real nervous look about him as he was only in his early twenties. He looked real disturbed from being there. I asked him what was wrong other than being locked up and not wanting to be here. He said someone told him that with his charges, he was going to prison. I told him to stop talking to everyone about his case because none of the guys in our dorm was an attorney. I asked him if he knew Jesus Christ. He said he had given his life to Christ in the past but backslid. I knew Jesus was an attorney and could change his life. He had done it for me, so surely, He could do it for this young guy in front of me. I began to witness to him and reminded him about Jesus Christ being the savior. I asked him if he would rededicate his life back to Christ, and he said yes! I was so excited and told him I would be right back.

I didn't think I knew what to do so stepped away to ask my Christian brother for help. I told him what happened and I needed him to come over to my bunk. I was certain my brother could lead him in rededicating his life back to Christ. I didn't want to screw it up and have him not say the right thing. I already had him standing there waiting for me to come back. I'm so glad he didn't change his mind while he was waiting. My brother says to me, "you got it, you know what to do."

I was nervous like "what, you not coming to help!" I couldn't just leave him standing there any longer alone so I went back and had him repeat after me: "I rededicate my life back to You, Jesus. I am a sinner, and I believe You died on the cross and rose from the dead." The Lord brought it to my attention later that when the young man said, "Jesus I'm a sinner and I rededicate my life back to you," it was already done, because he spoke from his heart.

**If you confess with your mouth the Lord Jesus and believe in your heart that God has raised Him from the dead, you will be saved. For with the heart one believes unto righteousness, and with the mouth confession is made unto salvation.** *(Romans 10:9-10)*

The young man began to attend some of the bible studies that I somehow ended up leading. It seemed all prayer calls and bible studies were first initiated by someone else but ended up falling on me to continue. I didn't know why I had to be responsible to keep this going, but saw the need. I just felt if I didn't do it, I was doing opposite of what God had wanted me to do. So, there it was!

This same guy had a court date approaching soon and I talked to him about fasting. I showed him in the bible how fasting would increase his faith in God and he was willing to give up something he loved to build his faith.

**Because of your unbelief; for assuredly, I say to you, if you have faith as a mustard seed, you will say to this mountain, move from here to there, and it will move; and nothing will be impossible for you. However, this kind does not go out except by prayer and fasting.** *(Matthew 17:20-21)*

The young man and his buddy both fasted from food and water for a complete twenty-four hours just as Jesus told His disciples as reported by Matthew. This too was a first time for them and they eagerly awaited midnight for an after the fast snack. It was truly hilarious, but they set their mind and overcame. I was so very proud of them.

The young man who rededicated his life went to court the next day and received probation over a prison sentence. This was awesome because it showed him that it didn't matter what anyone else says; the Lord has the final say. The Lord really moved on his behalf and once again showed me why I should trust Him. I began to see why obedience was better than sacrifice. These guys both obeyed what the Holy Spirit said through me and we all fasted together in agreement that this guy was going home. The outcome, one man released and another victory for Jesus!

My Christian brother who had become what I would have considered a friend and mentor was shipped out in the middle of the night. I never had the chance to say, "be safe" which means take care out there. I was grateful for meeting him and for getting to read the books by Joyce Meyer and Smith Wigglesworth. He had taught me some things and encouraged me to put my confidence in God. I appreciated him very much as our meeting was divine. He left a message for me to read a prayer to receive the baptism of the Holy Spirit. I remembered as a kid, my mother had me praying to receive the baptism of the Holy Spirit but I don't ever remember uttering a word. Even though I may have said the prayer, I don't remember wanting this gift as a child. If I desired the gift that would have meant I was surrendering myself to the Lord and I was not volunteering that yet. This time in my life, I was volunteering with both hands and feet up as if to say, "pick me Lord!!!"

I attempted to utter words and immediately began to pray in tongues and knew the devil had no idea what I was saying. These prayers were going straight to the Father and Satan couldn't do anything to stop it. When I pray in tongues, the Holy Spirit is interceding on my behalf. This powerful tool and weapon is very much needed in our daily Christian walk.

I was continuously being equipped and I welcomed it. Because I had an up and coming court date for probation violation, I would fast for another two and a half days with no food and water. This time however would be different because I now was able to pray in the spirit.

When I arrived at court, my probation officer wouldn't even look at me. I knew then something was up. My previous experience with this probation officer wasn't bad, but I knew, just had a feeling, any violation he would seek punishment–period point blank!

I had to have a separate trial for probation violation because it was regarding a previous offense which was separate from the new offense. The judge gave me two years cut in half to one year which would run concurrent with the previous sentence of four months given in the DUI trial. This meant I shouldn't do any more than a year including the time already spent in the county jail.

The outcome was still not what I had hoped but I kept my head high and believed in my heart that God was going to do something big on my behalf. I felt God knew something regarding me that only could be developed in me going away for a while; I just didn't know what it was. He had withheld this information! I didn't want to go but had no choice, just had to be willing to go through!

To my surprise, after being gone a couple of weeks, my brother that shipped out returned to the dorm. He had to go to another county to resolve some old issues. It didn't matter to me. I was just glad to see him and we resumed in our studies until I shipped out to prison.

My time at Wake County jail had now came to an end and I was off to the state processing prison camp in Goldsboro, North Carolina.

When I reflect on my time in Wake County jail, not only did my life change, but I also saw other lives change when faith was put in Jesus Christ. I've seen some people stop believing or even trying to believe due to not getting their desired outcome in court.

The truth is, we must hold on to our faith in Jesus Christ no matter what. This race is not for the swift and is for those that can persevere. It is not always easy but it is well worth it.

The Bible says when we leave our old lives for Him and the gospel, we not only receive eternal life with Him, but we also receive a hundredfold here on earth. A hundredfold is receiving the greatest return possible for what we have sown. This basically means when we sow our lives unto God we reap a blessed harvest in every area of our lives here on earth.

> **Therefore, if anyone is in Christ, he is a new creation; old things have passed away; behold, all things have become new.**
> *(2 Corinthians 5:17)*

The place I entered bound, I am now leaving free. In Christ, I am free indeed.

# Stepping out on Faith

     Under ordinary circumstances, inmates are transported from county jail to prison in a bus. But on this occasion, I was being transported in a car with one other person. It would seem the car would be more comfortable; however, having our feet shackled and hands shackled behind our backs for more than an hour drive was the most uncomfortable ride I've ever had. I had to constantly remind myself to remain calm, because, one day, this would all be over.

     Three days before my thirty-sixth birthday, I was on my way to prison. Neuse Correctional Center in Goldsboro, North Carolina was my destination. Upon arrival, I realized even more I didn't want to be here; yet, I had to go through this process. My feelings were a little mixed up because all I kept hearing from guys in the county was prison was so much better than jail. The food is much better and you even get to lift weights. You can also get a job which helps to reduce your time.

     In my mind, whether it be jail or prison, I was still locked up. There was no excitement at all in me about going to prison. I was trying my best not to complain about the repercussions from my own decision making.

     After being checked in, I realized there was an abundance of two things in this camp, flies and gnats. They were outside, in the dorm, and even more in the chow hall. If you looked away from your food for one second, you might look back and see it being airlifted by a very large fly. Going on an absolute fast, crossed my mind on many occasions. The little things taken for granted become major desires when you don't have them. Eating my food without swatting my food every five seconds was a strong desire of mine at this point.

     My focus was solely on being obedient, being patient and speaking to my counselor. To get a conversation with my counselor was worth all the canteen I had.

     The county jail was so full of inmates imitating themselves as lawyers who would tell you how your case would go and how much time you would get to only be wrong about their own cases. Some were even there longer than they expected and yet would always have something to say.

You couldn't help but hear what others said from experience, but I just preferred to hear it from the horse's mouth whom happened to be my counselor.

After finally speaking with my counselor there was confusion in the system with my case. The system showed I had a two-year sentence which was not the truth. Wake County Clerk of Courts was behind on their work and had yet to update the system to reflect the correct information. As far as my counselor could see, I had a long way to go before release. Not Cool!!!

Being new at serving God was a trying process. I wondered at times if the Lord was hearing my petitions. I wanted answers but had to wait. I just wanted to know my real release date so I could have something to lock in my brain. Not knowing was working me but what could I do. I guess this situation was adding to my patience resume.

**Now this is the confidence that we have in Him, that if we ask anything according to His will, He hears us. And if we know that He hears us, whatever we ask, we know that we have the petitions that we have asked of Him.** *(1 John: 14-15)*

For a first-time experience, this was not going the way I had hoped. I wanted things one way but they were being served in a different manner. I was beginning to see what trusting God was all about.

I was being re-molded and my thought process was being recreated. I had to trust God not with my own understanding but with all that surpasses my understanding. He is truly the answer and the way! Even if I didn't know, He knows, so I must be patient and follow His lead even in the middle of my discouragement. In Him there's peace like a river.

I was also learning when I say, "I trust Him," not to be a hypocrite. Worrying all the time and always being discouraged would prove that I did not trust God as much as I say I did. Actions always speak louder than words.

In the Goldsboro processing prison, I did not have access to the weight pile. I had to do as I did in the county jail and use my own body. Push-ups, dips and crunches are my daily routine. I wanted my physical body to go through a transformation just as my spirit man had. I enjoyed working out. It was refreshing and a sense of release for some built-up feelings and emotions.

Spending time with my new best friend Jesus was more important than anything else. Oh, how I love Jesus! His Word just ignites me when I read and meditate on it. It prompted me to focus on good things even though with my natural eye a bad place was in view.

> **And now, brothers, as I close this letter, let me say this one more thing: Fix your thoughts on what is true and good and right. Think about things that are pure and lovely, and dwell on the fine, good things in others. Think about all you can praise God for and be glad about. Keep putting into practice all you learned from me and saw me doing, and the God of peace will be with you.**
>
> *(Philippians 4:8-9, The Living Bible)*

In the middle of all of this, I received a second letter from my girlfriend. It had now been over a month since she had written me. I had spoken to her one time on a three-way call that my mother dialed for me. I reached out to her several other times; however, she only answered once. I wasn't sure if she was working or just didn't want to talk to me. I was hoping she would visit but had not. Honestly when I received the letter from her again, I didn't know what to expect. As I began to read, to my surprise it was all about how much she missed me and loved me. Her words sounded good, and what I'd been wanting to hear from her since the beginning of me being away. By this time, I felt a little reluctant to give in to the emotions. I thought I was setting myself up for disappointment. It did feel good to be thought of by her though.

In my waiting, I knew what I had to do. Every time that chapel was open to Christian services I would be ready to go in. The chapel allowed services for many different religions including Islam for the Muslims.

I had to check the calendar to ensure when to go and when not to go. No disrespect to anyone and their beliefs, but my eyes were on Jesus and I couldn't allow anything else contrary to Him in my spirit.

Often, I had a lot of free time on my hand; so, I tried to make wise use of it. Being that I was in unfamiliar territory, I prayed and asked the Lord to send me a new Christian brother that loved God and spoke truth. Someone, who would help me in my growing process.

After having conversations with different people, I could sense that not everyone who professed Jesus Christ was always sincere about their relationship with Him. In this stage of my life, I needed sincerity.

It didn't matter that we were in prison because the truth is I was in a mental prison before ever stepping foot into an actual physical prison. I didn't become free until I gave my life to Christ.

This place was so much different than the county jail as it was wide open and so much movement from the inmates. Whether we were inside or outside the dorms I had to quickly adjust to what was happening around me because safety was first while standing my ground in who I am. You never knew because people fought and people had made shanks or knives and being careful was not only wise but it was a part of daily survival.

I was now living a new life with a new belief system. I was serving a new God, Jesus! My old god was the streets. I was not the same guy and every day it showed itself. My talk was different, my walk had changed. I still saw myself as a cool dude but this was transition for me, especially being behind bars. I cussed all the time and clung to whatever held my attention. Cigarettes were being sold to who ever wanted to smoke. In my old life participating with them would be mandatory. But not now, I was done with that!

One day I was sitting outside reading my bible and this dude walked up to me and started having a conversation about the Lord. I didn't know what discernment was at the time but my senses said this guy was my answered prayer. We hung out on the yard, studied and sometimes worked out together. He began to teach me the difference between reading and studying. He advised me to work on retaining scripture.

This made me a little nervous because I thought he was saying I needed to memorize the entire bible, but that was not what he was saying at all. He was referring to practice retaining scripture without looking at the bible to see it. I wanted to hide the Word of God in my heart so I would just meditate on it. I asked the Lord to help me with this. I would practice saying scripture out loud and repeating until I could say without looking at the paper. I learned through this process that even though I spend time in the Word, I may not always remember every scripture or verse or even the book it's in. But the Holy Spirit will bring back to my remembrance what I have hidden in my heart. The Word of God sustains me and I don't want to forget it.

**But the Helper, the Holy Spirit, whom the Father will send in My name, He will teach you all things, and bring to your remembrance all things that I said to you.** *(John 14:26)*

It was weird not having prayer call before lights out after count cleared. Count was when the officers had to count everybody and make sure everyone was present and accounted for. We weren't cleared until all were where they were supposed to be. I got accustomed to this time that I believed God had ordained for me to be a part of. Prison setup was different than the county jail. I looked around and it appeared to me that no one would even want to participate, so for a couple of days, I said nothing. Even though I prayed and studied on my own, I felt the Holy Spirit was nudging me to announce a prayer call. I kept telling myself they don't want it but the Holy Spirit was telling me to call it. I felt as nervous as I did in the county, even more so than when the responsibility seemed to fall in my lap. The county was intramural, more small time, but prison was the big leagues. The Holy Spirit would not let up off me. It even got uncomfortable to stand in the count lineup but I kept right on fighting Him. God won and I lost; so, I finally gave in.

I got the nerve to ask someone if I called a prayer call would anyone be interested because I noticed there was not one being held. The response I received was, "If you call it I'll come." "WOW!!!" I had said, "they didn't want it," but the Lord knew there were some waiting for the opportunity to pray as a group and make their requests known.

You can never count anyone out or think because they don't act like you or talk like you, that they don't want prayer or are not looking for God. Many wanted God but because they may be judged by their outer appearance or past mistakes they keep their mouths shut. I had to repent and ask for forgiveness. I remembered I was also in prison and they may have even been skeptical of me. I was still dealing with my own insecurities of worthiness to be used by God and doubting if I would be received by the people. It had to be orchestrated by God and not me. I called my first prayer call in prison, and some guys participated.

One guy even asked for a special prayer request regarding his family. I prayed for him and he said he really needed it. What If I stayed stuck in my own fears and observations and kept my mouth closed. That guy would have been stressing about something that God wanted to fix on his behalf. He needed an intercessor and I became that for him. I could see a weight being lifted off him while I was praying. He didn't judge me for being in prison and it was as if he knew the Lord heard me and would answer my prayers. Even now I pray, "Lord, forgive me for judging people. You are the one who draws them to Your son Jesus not me. I'm just the vessel used." In John 6:44, Jesus said, "No one can come to Me unless the Father who sent me draws him." This would be the first of many prayer calls, I would lead and I always felt good and free after each one in doing my assignment. It was a joy to see others gain a sense of peace because of prayer, including me.

There was a young guy who came in for processing and his bunk was right over mine. I spent time on my bunk whenever it was too hot outside as the flies were more tolerable in the dorm. I read and studied a lot by myself. This new guy was real shy and had knowledge of God but was avoiding Him. He had been pushed by his family to give his life to Christ and because of this, he rebelled. It's funny how all the years in the pushing he rebelled but whenever I opened my bible, he voluntarily sat right there and listened. He always wanted to talk and listen. I never tried to push him or persuade him; I just shared the gospel as I was learning and receiving revelation. His family planted the seed. My assignment was to water the seed but with a different approach. The Lord got the increase of the harvest because after conversations and the Holy Spirit having His way, he finally said to me he wanted to accept Jesus Christ as his Lord and Savior. Another WOW!!! Again, the Lord used me to bring someone to Him. I was still blown away that the Holy Spirit was using someone like me to do a work for Him. To see this guy come to Christ was absolutely amazing. The devil has lost another one. To God be all the glory!

Late that same night, I got a tap on my bunk by one of the correctional officers telling me to get my stuff together because I was shipping out. This meant I am now done with processing and on my way to a new prison camp. This was at no notice, no warning and no time to say goodbye to any of the other brothers. I've been here a total of 18 days and now it's time to go.

Looking back, I know I was in my own process but God also had me on assignment. I didn't know that then and now I see why our yes to Him is so important. It's not just to secure us but to also be of influence to others so that they can be secured in Him as well.

Thank you Lord for keeping me, and for those You connected me with.

New undisclosed place, here I come.

# Up Against the Wall

Well now it's official. No more processing camp! I've just arrived at my new temporary residence in Sanford, North Carolina. My main concern was, I'm hoping the flies and gnats aren't as bad as where I just came from in Goldsboro. Even in this uncomfortable situation, please Lord, let all the worrisome bugs not be here. The Lord answered that prayer for me. They're here but they're not as bad. Thank you, Jesus!

After getting checked in and getting settled, I realized the environment was different. Nothing about this place felt right. There was an uneasiness in my spirit. As I was supplied my daily prison clothes, I was not feeling this part of the process at all. Mostly all the prison clothes and undergarments were recycled. My first set of clothes were dingy white boxers, dingy white socks and dingy white t-shirts. Basically, I had to wear drawers that someone else had worn. This was straight bull jive! What a miserable feeling! Talking about having a life readjustment! In processing, I started out with mostly all new clothing, so it was not as bad. This is straight unsanitary! Don't these guys know these drawers are unclean? Is anyone really expecting me to wear these? Seriously!!

Only the Lord knew, at this moment, I needed supernatural strength and the willingness to endure. Only He could give me such strength to get through and cooperate without a fight. I couldn't be a complainer because this was a part of my process and the repercussion to what I had done. However, this was the worst, I can't lie!

After getting settled, I ran into a brother I recognized from church services held at the Neuse processing camp where I had just left in Goldsboro. He came up to me and introduced himself and told me about a prayer service being held that night in the chow hall. Being my first night at a new camp, prayer was exactly what I needed to get this started right, especially after that dirty clothes incident.

After attending prayer, I felt so much better. Although in the presence of God in prayer, I came to realize I didn't understand my circumstance.

However, I would be patient and trust in God. I didn't like it here but I knew there was a plan for me that I couldn't see. I knew I had to stay in my Word and have a joyful spirit while my ark was being built. In the bible God told Noah to build an ark. This ark was to keep Noah and everybody in the ark safe while the outside world was being destroyed. Noah would soon stand on new ground and have a new beginning. The things that had been my norm I was being detached from and I was soon to stand on new ground and have a new beginning. I just had to weather the storm!

This camp did not have a chapel so worship services were held in the chow hall. It was hot all the time in there because the air didn't work. The guys had electric fans hooked up just to keep it somewhat cool and halfway comfortable. I had to find peace in all of this because it was very uncomfortable.

I was grateful I met some of the other Christian believers at the camp who gave me the 411 on how the camp was run. I learned about other nightly services and groups like Yokefellow who come out regularly. Yokefellow is a prison ministry where a group of Christians on the outside chose to be yoked in fellowship with those on the inside to share about faith in God, direction and each one's purpose. This was awesome and just another way I experienced the love of God through His people.

I had an opportunity to meet the prison chaplain. In that meeting, he told me about a baptism being held within the next few days. I was eager to be a participant. I remember being baptized as a child but this would be so much different. I wanted it! I knew it symbolized my new walk of life in Jesus. I was willing to do anything and everything to let the Lord know I was serious about walking with Him. I'm excited because not much longer after arriving at the camp, I was baptized. It felt so good inside and even others were being baptized as well. It felt like I was a part of a unique John the Baptist experience being baptized in prison because this place was like the wilderness.

I knew then Jesus was on this camp operating in others as well; and it was a privilege to be a part of such an event. This was the kind of service that no one from the outside would ever see. No cameras, just willing men wanting to have their lives turned around by Jesus Christ. No one could ever tell me that Jesus is not real! He is real and very much alive. I could see Him in others and most importantly I could feel and see Him in me. I left the old me at the bottom of that baptismal pool. This new place I'm in is different, so very different! My time in Sanford is only temporary and I will leave here one day sooner than I know, so I'll be ok. This is my journey, this is my process!

    Within a week of getting there, I was granted an appointment to speak with my counselor. I was nervous at first because I didn't know what to expect going in. On my way to the counselor's office I overheard my favorite childhood song by the Clark Sisters "I'm looking for a Miracle," playing in a nearby office.

*I'm looking for a miracle*
*I expect the impossible*
*I feel the intangible and*
*I see the invisible*

*The Sky is the limit*
*To what I can have*

*Just believe and receive it*
*God will perform it today*
*Hey, Hey, ay*
*Just believe and receive it*
*God will perform it today*

*I'm looking for a miracle*
*I expect the impossible*
*I feel the intangible and*
*I see the invisible*

*The Sky is the limit*
*To what I can have*

*Just believe and receive it*
*God will perform it today*
*Hey, Hey, ay*
*Just believe and receive it*
*God will perform it today*

*I expect a miracle every day,*
*God will make a way out of no way*

*Just believe and receive it*
*God will perform it today*
*Hey, Hey, ay*
*Just believe and receive it*
*God will perform it today*

*(Clark Sisters, "I'm Looking for a Miracle")*

All I could do was smile and sing to myself as I knew the Lord was speaking to me through that song. I walked in the counselor's building not knowing what to expect but after that encounter on the way to her office, I was left expecting a miracle.

My counselor here told me the same thing that the counselor said back at the Neuse. I tried to not let that bring me down; why am I showing to be released in two years? I just wanted to be alone with God for a moment and talk to Him. It seemed like so much was going on around me and at times, I just felt stuck. Where was my miracle?

Because this was a minimum-security prison, we lived in open dormitories. The guy that slept on the bottom bunk below me seemed to be cool, except he would always leave his locker door open when I was around. On the inside of his locker door were pictures of almost naked girls. Even though I had my moments, I was trying not to think about sex. Seriously though, I was a highly sexual active man on the streets but I'm in prison and more than that I'm saved. This was not just time away for my punishment, but I was also being cleansed mentally and spiritually and even physically.

This is where I begin learning to play the "look away game." Whenever I saw the pictures, I looked away. Sometimes I did pretty good, and other times, wasn't quite so easy. I wanted to see them but it was unhealthy. I could feel I was being watched. It was like people were identifying who I was, not personally but spiritually. It was weird!

I wasn't trying to impress anyone; I just wanted to keep my focus on God. I tried not to be stressed and worried because when I did I wasn't focusing on Him. Truth be told, I did not like this place! It appeared to have a dark cloud over it. I figured if I stayed to myself and stayed in the Word of God that my time would fly by.

I found out if I got a job, I could work some time off my sentence. For that you could count me all in. I figured since I didn't know my exact release date, I might as well work off what I could. Whenever the system finally updated, I would be negative some time and this would work towards my benefit. I was told a job in the kitchen was the highest paid job without leaving the camp and would also give me more credit. For this reason, I applied.

I got the kitchen job and because I did, I had to move from my old dorm to the kitchen dorm. This meant no more naked girls from my bunk mate! I was excited about this new place. You'd have thought I was being released and in a way, I was. I was sure there were a couple of guys in the dorm that I was in at first who didn't like me, even though they didn't know me. Sometimes a person doesn't have to say it; you can just sense it. This was my discernment kicking in; even though, I didn't know it at the time.

On the new job, I was placed on the morning crew to feed breakfast and lunch for three hundred inmates. I had to get up every morning at 2:30 a.m. to be in the kitchen at 3:00 a.m.

I started off working as a dishwasher making $1.20 a week. I never appreciated the value of a dollar until working at this wage. It really caused me to look back on all the money I misused and failed to steward over well. I told myself I would no longer misuse the finances God would release into my hands.

As the bible says in the book of Matthew, chapter 25, I want to be considered by God as faithful over small things and then He will trust me with big things.

I wasn't really trying to make friends. I just wanted to handle my business and get out when my time was up. A lot of the guys in my dorm worked the kitchen just on different shifts. I had no choice but to have conversation with some of them because we had to work together as a team.

You can often tell where a person is by talking to them. You can get their beliefs, the moral code they live by, mostly through conversation. The rest you can stand back, watch and see. In prison, you can do your thing, whatever that is, but always keep a watchful eye on your surroundings.

No matter what we do we have to move through the eyes of God or we'll get tripped up. The enemy plans sneak attacks; and we can't allow ourselves to be careless and get caught off guard. I speak right now according to the Word of God, no weapon formed against the people of God, no matter where they are in their lives or current circumstances shall prosper in Jesus mighty name.

Like everywhere else I was confined to, I spent as much time in the Word as I could. Every time I opened my bible, it felt as if I was opening the details of my new Identity. My success was all detailed in the bible, which is the voice of God. My peace, my victory, my standard of relationships, my everything was all in my heavenly Father through Jesus Christ. I can't survive life without Jesus Christ and I am so grateful that I can walk in the strength that only comes from Him. I was living a supernatural life and didn't even realize it. I was blessed supernaturally, covered supernaturally and was overcoming obstacles supernaturally. These are things that I couldn't possibly have done on my own. When God allows something to happen on our behalf that we couldn't cause by ourselves, it is supernatural. He is a supernatural God. Nothing about Him is regular or ordinary. The strength to get through this time in my life was beyond normal. I could endure only because of His presence. The consequences of my actions brought me into the arms of my heavenly Father and I wouldn't trade that for anything.

The guy who told me about the prayer service introduced me to some of the guys that had a regular bible study on the prison yard every day. There were about six to eight guys meeting up at a picnic table to learn more about the Word of God and our position of function in this relationship.

This was where I was told by one of the brothers, I had to step up my tools. My tools I was told would be the things I used to study God's Word with. I had a small basic bible that I would carry everywhere. It was recommended I get a Dake Study Bible if I could. I didn't know who Dake was, but he came highly recommended by someone who seemed to be knowledgeable of the Word.

I reached out to my mother back home and made my petition. Not too much longer, I not only received my Dake Study Bible in the mail, but it was even engraved with my name on the front cover. I was excited because I now had an upgraded tool to work with in my learning.

I also saw it as beneficial to the other brothers who would attend our studies. This new bible was difficult to put down. It contained so much information to study. Alongside the Word, it contained commentary and a dictionary and even maps of biblical travels. There was a wealth of information that I never knew existed or could have even dared to dream now at my fingertips. This took my mind off the wait of a release date. In the meantime, I found out how to write to Wake County to get an update on my sentence so I did.

I am really learning what it means to have patience. I feel it would have been somewhat disrespectful to Jesus not to have patience in my wait. My heavenly Father waited 35 years before I truly confessed Him as my Lord and Savior, so 2 years to His 35 is not long at all. In my wait, I had one goal and that was to learn all I could about my new God and what my place was in conjunction. I spent so much time serving Satan in the past, it was time for a makeover in my mind, heart and spirit.

It bothered me that I didn't know a lot of scripture by heart so one of the brothers gave me and a couple others some scriptures to practice memorizing. One of the scriptures was in 2 Corinthians.

**For godly sorrow produces repentance leading to salvation, not to be regretted; but the sorrow of the world produces death.**
*(2 Corinthians 7:10)*

When the things we've done in this world bring us despair, and from that despair we repent and ask the Lord for forgiveness, we are changing our minds to live for Him versus living that old life. We are doing this at no matter the cost for us. Sorrow of the world basically means we are just sorry we got caught and not because we want inner change. This kind of sorrow brings spiritual death which is a separation from God leading ultimately to eternal death which is being separated forever.

This reminds me of time I spent in the county jail. Some guys would join the prayer circle to pray but once they were sentenced to prison or received an outcome different than what they'd prayed for they would then stop praying and acknowledging God. They wanted nothing more to do with Him and that was not right as well as selfish. They were only praying to get something for their personal benefit but it was never intended in their heart to pray for a new relationship with God. They didn't want to give up their old lives for a new one with Him. To be honest, I had done this myself many times before. This was not cool at all and only shows a leach mentality. Let me get what I can, and if you have nothing that I want then I'm gone.

We were also given this scripture from Acts.

**Repent therefore and be converted, that your sins may be blotted out, so that times of refreshing may come from the presence of the Lord.** *(Acts 3:19)*

This is about changing our mind and attitude toward God so that He could clean us of the old and refresh us with His presence. He refreshes with His love and forgiveness. He restores us to our rightful place and makes all things new in our lives. We are revitalized in Him. He nourishes our soul.

I even learned this verse from Romans:

**And do not be conformed to this world, but be transformed by the renewing of your mind, that you may prove what is that good and acceptable and perfect will of God.** *(Romans 12:2)*

Coming to Christ gives a new way of living and it is the only way of true satisfaction. We are not to repeat or emulate a life not in Christ if we want to succeed in the things of Him. Allow the Holy Spirit to change our hearts and mind. He will also give us a new viewpoint and perspective on life and what living is surely all about.

As I began to say these scriptures over and over, revelation began to come and it registered in my spirit how the Holy Spirit wants to be our motivation for living. We always have help and are never alone.

I really love Jesus and I just wanted to prove that I was loyal to Him. I wanted Him to know that He could count on me to follow Him. I wanted Him to know how much I loved Him and wanted to learn all I could about Him. I want to be a better man and to become one with His spirit. I wanted Him to know I was there for Him when the whole time He was showing me He was there for me. I screw up at times and am not always as loyal as I should be. I don't always have my mind in the right place; yet, He was showing me His loyalty.

One of the brothers told me to always remain humble due to the anointing on my life. I didn't know what it meant to be anointed. I knew there was a change in me but was not clear on anointing or even being chosen. The bible says, "Many are called but few are chosen." To be given power and authority to do something God chose me to do was mind-blowing. Me! He chose me! I am a former drug dealer, a former addict. I was a liar and a womanizer. I was a whore who thought it nothing more than manly to sleep with as many women as possible, more than one in a day and even two at the time on different occasions! I had so many faulty characteristics about myself, I could go on and on naming them. Yet He called me! I was called before but didn't answer.

This time, was I going to make that same mistake again? I think not! His blood wiped away all those things about me that kept disqualifying me from life in Him. As a matter of fact, He wanted me because of all the things I had done in my lifetime. I was the kind of guy He was looking for.

**Those who are well have no need of a physician, but those who are sick...For I did not come to call the righteous, but sinners, to repentance.** *(Matthew 9:12-13)*

His blood purified me! He took the old Dimitri, made me new and then dressed me in fresh new attire. That is how much He loves me. How much He loves us. No matter what has been committed He can reconstruct those things all for His glory. He takes those that the world would throw away and makes them beautiful and then the world would envy their life. This is for His praise and His glory! Knowing He chose me takes me to a place of humility. I have value, says the Lord. I am worth something and so are you says the Lord! Being brought into the knowledge of Christ makes things not as bad as they may seem.

Occasionally, when I would go to the clothes house to get supposedly fresh clothes after I've traded in the dirty clothes, I would sometimes get a pair of new boxers, socks and t-shirts. I was told by one of the guys in my dorm to keep them and wash them with the bar of soap we used to clean our bodies. This soap would dry your skin out something terrible but had some type of properties in it to make everything white. What was once a problem, is now no more. What seemed big was brought down to size. Even in this, the Lord was helping me to adjust and to overcome. In Him, there is always provision. This taught me a valuable lesson. Don't sweat the small stuff.

As a matter of fact, don't sweat the big stuff either! They are all considered small to an Omnipotent God meaning, He's all powerful! Nothing is greater than God, not a circumstance, a situation and most definitely not a prison sentence! I trust in the Lord! I trust in the Lord! Say it out loud with me, I trust in the Lord!

# Game Time

> But those who wait on the Lord shall renew their strength; they shall mount up with wings like eagles, they shall run and not be weary, they shall walk and not faint. *(Isaiah 40:31)*

The word "wait" was now becoming a common word in my daily language. I received a response letter from Wake County regarding my time. They basically said, they received my request and to be patient while the system is being updated. In other words, WAIT Dimitri! What are my options here? I'll wait.

There must be purpose in all of this. I felt deep down inside when the system caught up with itself my name would be called for me to pack my stuff and go to the gate because I was going home. I could see it every day in my mind and I was excited. I knew it would happen soon, I just didn't know when and because of that I must get ready. I realized in life when we are anticipating a next leg of our journey we must get ready for it. Don't wait until that bigger moment comes, get prepared for it now, as if you already have it. Greatness is not the fruit of the big moment. Greatness is established in the process. The big moment is just the manifestation of the greatness already seen.

That is not just a change in the physical but also a change in our thinking. We can no longer think like the current situation, we must train our thoughts to think beyond where we are right now. That transformation, mind renewal and faith only comes from the Word of God.

I began to clear my mind of the past and even of the present by walking and even listening to Christian radio. We were permitted to have little transistor radios with headphones to pick up whatever radio stations would come through. I could never really get a clear signal of THE LIGHT radio station which is a gospel station that I was familiar with back home in Raleigh. I would always pick up a station I'd never heard of before called,

HIS RADIO. HIS RADIO was what I considered a contemporary Christian music station. Some of the songs I would hear I recognized from when I was a lot younger.

At one point in my life, I attended a church with my mother called, Grace Covenant Church in Rocky Mount, North Carolina, where I'm originally from. This church had a mixed congregation but was predominately white. Everybody there was real cool and I honestly loved the church. I wasn't living right even though I attended some youth groups and played the drums there for a short stint. I still however felt as if I was a part of the people. Their song selection was different than your typical black Baptist church like the one I went to as a kid.

I also loved Ebenezer Baptist Church because I had a lot of friends there. That's where I sang in the tot choir or children's choir as a young kid.

I was never against church. I just didn't want to give up my worldly freedoms. I preferred to do as Dimitri pleased. So sometimes I went to church; I just didn't follow the Christian lifestyle.

At this moment in time, this music coming through my radio was exactly what I needed. It was encouraging and soothing. There were times I could get a good signal for THE LIGHT radio station and would mix it up a little. I was being molded and developed so no matter what, I knew I had to be careful at what I listened to.

I also knew I had to do something with my body. When I was arrested I weighed 218 lbs. at 5'8" and some change. I drank a lot of alcohol so had more body fat than muscle. I saw one of the fellas from the bible study table working out alone in the corner of the prison yard. I went to him and asked him if he would help me get in shape. He had been in prison a lot longer than I had and was really fit. He told me about his boxing training and that he would help me but most people who asked they just don't last too long in his workouts. He said he would only help me out if I was serious about getting in shape. I told him I had no other option and quitting was not a choice of mine. I was in it to win it.

Our workout began right then and there and he immediately began to work the crap out of me. He made me want to quit but I knew I couldn't. His focus was on working the body by using only the body and very little weights and even then, only occasionally. We trained just as hard if not harder than someone who uses weights as the primary tool. Fighting and enduring through the pain helped my mind to settle and become sharper. We did a lot of jumping jacks or side straddle hops as we called them in the United States Marine Corps.

During this exercise he would yell at me, and ask, who's my best friend? My response was always Jesus! I was being trained not only physically but also spiritually as I often called on the Lord during these gruesome workouts. Because I was no longer getting high, smoking and drinking, my body responded to the workouts and I began to drop weight.

I knew God had to be watching out for me because I looked up one day while working out on the yard and saw three white doves.

**And the Holy Spirit descended in bodily form like a dove upon Him, and a voice came from heaven which said, "You are My beloved Son; in You I am well pleased."** *(Luke 3:22)*

When I saw that, I was like, "yoooo," I know God got me covered! He even sent the doves to give me a sign! I didn't know at the time much about the doves but I knew that they had something to do with God and I believed they were there for me. It gave me peace that day like all was well. The dove represents the Holy Spirit and that was very comforting to see them in the number of the trinity. God has a way of showing Himself that keeps amazing me more and more each day.

I got a promotion in the kitchen and was now working as the prep cook. This position is right under the head cook. I was now making about $4.90 a week. More responsibility brought more money and I was grateful. I had to prepare the food to be cooked such as hand peeling and dicing potatoes for potato salad to feed about 300 inmates. I made large quantities of coleslaw and even sorted through many 100 lb bags of beans and peas to remove the dead ones and even rocks so I could soak and prepare them for meals.

Chopping and dicing for this amount of people was a beast all by itself. The knife I was given to use was always locked up to a table so I or anyone else wouldn't "accidentally" walk away with it.

I was finally getting adjusted to prison and my daily life. My days consisted of kitchen duties, bible study with the fellas, working out and attending any church services being held, plus I had my own personal study time. I was trying to stay focused and then I received an unexpected letter in the mail.

I always got mail from different people but I was not looking for this one. It was a letter from my girl. This letter was a lot different from the second letter as it was all about what she was going through in hard times. Her stepfather had passed away and she was not taking it well. This really bothered me and I wished I could have been there for her. Her mother was not doing well either. My girl was dealing heavy with this and on top of everything else going on in her life; so, I began to pray for strength, peace and comfort for her and her family. I didn't know what the death of a parent felt like, but was familiar of the pain of losing a loved one. From experience, it was a deep place that would be hard to get out of without support. This kind of pain does not feel good at all.

Setting all this aside for a moment, I accepted she and I were no longer together. I prayed for us and I prayed for her a lot. Things in me were dying and it seemed almost obvious my new life was not going to include her. This was not by my choice, it was just the way the pieces were falling. As much as it hurt, I was slowly beginning to accept it and be ok with it.

My desire was for her to be happy and in a good place spiritually. I wanted her to know Jesus Christ personally as Lord and Savior. She wasn't a bad person, and I would have bet, if He could turn me around, the bad sinner, He could surely for her do the same. If she could experience His love the way I did or just become aware of His love already being present, it would change her life forever. He had been there the whole time, but I just couldn't see it. I didn't recognize how much He had given of Himself for me. She just needed a special revelation of Him. I prayed she receives it. This would be the final letter I received from her for the duration of my time within this parenthesis.

Jesus Christ is amazing! My heart is to share Him with everyone who has an ear to hear and a heart to receive. I know what it's like to want to run away from the "Christian folk" because I did it. You don't want to hear about going to hell for all the wrong doings and jacked up lifestyle. I know, I get it.

There's so much to God that the message didn't always get spread correctly. Even though Hell is real, to get to know God is so comforting because He's not this mean person who wants to kill all the bad people. He's loving, kind, gentle and so forgiving. People like me who were considered bad in the world—He loves us. He wants to show everyone just how much. If you don't know Him personally allow Him to show you. Just say, "Show me Lord, who You are," and He will grant your request. No matter where we are in life He will show up and show off on our behalf. It makes His name great in the eyes of His children. He wants us to be proud of Him. He's great anyway and no one can take that away from Him, but it really hits home when we can recognize His greatness and want to be with Him.

At one of the church services I attended, it seemed it was a setup just for me. I had not really shown any outward emotions during this new walk while amongst other people because of where I was. This day here was a setup, man oh man, it was a setup. One of the ministers, to this day I have no clue his name or his ministry affiliation, called me out and began prophesying to me. All I remember was I began crying and couldn't stop saying, "Thank You Jesus, thank You Father, I am not worthy."

I never wanted to cry in prison especially in front of people. There were some of the guys at the church service who wanted to be nosy. Some felt they had nothing better to do. Some had just wanted to see the females when they came to visit. I didn't care who was there, who saw me or would talk about me. All I know is, I felt God hugging me right there in that prison and it was the best feeling in the world. Shedding tears that day broke something off me.

I was no longer caged in. I was truly open to be free in my walk and there's nothing like being free in Jesus.

One of the coolest days I've had in a long time was when I got my first visit on the yard from my Ma. This was a beautiful visit as she was so pretty. It seemed like she hadn't aged at all. I know she preferred me at home versus being in prison but I was ok and had to go through this process. I was growing and learning Jesus. I was also learning about me.

My mom is the best and I was so grateful for all the hot food she brought me. It was a long time since I had eaten some food from the street. All I can say is, if your mother is still alive, honor her as much as possible. Pray for your mom and try to be the best son or daughter you can because our time with them is limited. The bible says to honor thy mother and thy father. This honor also includes those who may not have physically birthed you but have held up the standard as a parent in your life.

My mom has always been there for me in all my life so I am thankful to the Lord for her. I gave her hell and she never walked away. I'm sure it wasn't easy for her at times but she never did, for that I am forever grateful. I love my mother and there will never be another her. I pray she lives a long and healthy life for the rest of her days.

All my life, I've been surrounded by truth. There is the truth of existence due to there being truth of a creator. There's truth of actions and consequences or as the bible says, sowing and reaping. Many times, I saw the truth of who I really was, not who I was made up to be. I would talk about the existence of God as if I knew Him personally but was still living a contradicting lifestyle. My inner man knew where my help came from, even though I ignored Him in my selfishness and did what I wanted. If we really take the time to stop and look around at all the things that concern us, God has been there and still is. Even when things have seemed to be their worst, God was there the whole time. Truth!!!

Once I became a believer even more truth became evident. Whenever I attended AA or Alcoholics Anonymous, we had to introduce ourselves, "hello my name is (give your name), I'm an alcoholic." My spirit man did not agree with what I was being told to say. Admittance is one thing but this was different for me. I don't knock the program or anything because many people have been helped and are still being helped every day because of the work put in by those at AA. My issue was as a believer of Jesus Christ, I agreed with the bible which says, I'm healed by the stripes Jesus took on my behalf. I said a prayer in the Wake County jail and asked for the taste of alcohol and drugs to be taken away from me. I believed it was done and I know without a shadow of doubt I was instantly delivered from these things. How could I still address myself as something I've already been delivered from? I'm healed so why call myself sick. I'm no longer an alcoholic and I will not claim that as my current state because I am no longer that man. I am a new man in Christ. Old things have passed away and all has become new. I was trying to follow their rules, but my spirit was not in agreement.

For us, who were believers, that was declaring a lie. One of the brothers who worked alongside the chaplain recognized this and spoke up about it at one of our studies at the picnic table. I was glad he did because he confirmed what I was feeling inside and believed to be truth. Don't call yourself what you're not unless you believe it.

We normally speak what we've been taught or experienced and I personally experienced the healing of God and was sure of my deliverance. I will not speak into the atmosphere the opposite as if it had not happened. That's like saying Jesus didn't go to the cross and wasn't raised from the dead three days later. He did and that's truth!!!

**He personally carried the load of our sins in His own body when He died on the cross so that we can be finished with sin and live a good life from now on. For His wounds have healed ours.** *(1 Peter 2:24, The Living Bible)*

To know what Jesus did on the cross to heal and deliver me makes my heart glad. He didn't just do it for me, He did it for you. It was all for the benefit of who will believe and receive. As a recipient of such love, I felt the need to handle people differently, with more kindness and compassion. I wanted to encourage anybody that crossed my path in whatever they were going through.

One day two guys I had occasionally conversed with were about to fight. This was an out of the ordinary day because all those who worked in the kitchen had to unload a couple of trucks that were dropping off food and produce. We had to stock the sheds and freezers with all this fresh food. There was a lot to be unloaded so it required even more help than just the kitchen crew. One of the guys, a really big country dude, from South Carolina, who had already done close to ten years, was coming to the end of his sentence this year. The guy he was about to fight had not been in that long and was more of a short timer like myself. I just so happened to walk up on them behind a shed about to throw down. They were the only two back there besides me; no one else knew they were back there. I know I must have been out of mind and before I was saved I would have just been like handle your business and go for what you know.

This new me spoke a different kind of boldness to say to them STOP!! I told them both they were close to getting out and neither wanted to mess that up by fighting over something that wasn't that serious. I knew I had violated the prison code and had opened my mouth up to something I was going to surely hear about later. They listened to me though and didn't fight.

However, the guy, from South Carolina was three times my size and looked like all he's been doing for ten years was lifting weights. He said something to some of his people and on my way back to the dorm, he saw me as I was about to walk in. His boys were also hanging around the door and then when I was about to walk in he told me I needed to mind my own business. We locked eyes but I felt in my spirit not to say anything. I wasn't afraid of him, however, he had a right to say what he said to me "so to speak."

I mean what could I have said to defend my reasoning for doing what I did? Should I have said I was lead, by the Holy Spirit? We weren't best friends or anything like that, and honestly, we barely even spoke to each other. I just knew what I knew through hearing him talk close by me occasionally. I felt compelled to speak up and try and prevent them both from making a big mistake.

Another guy he was cool with, the head cook that I worked under, spoke up for me and said, "D-Ray," which is what they called me, "was just trying to help." Our eyes were still locked on each other for approximately sixty seconds then the crowd disbursed. He went inside and we never discussed this situation again. He never had much to say to me after that.

That really could have turned out another way but God stepped in on my behalf. The Holy Spirit locked my jaws so I couldn't speak. I've learned at times it's best to not always respond. I've seen a couple of the other believers just go back and forth with some of these guys and it was all a bunch of nonsense. Some of these dudes in here just wanted to test folk and push their buttons to see how far they can go. Why argue with someone who feels they have nothing to lose. This is how some of us got here in the first place. I was never one to do a lot of back and forth, either we were or we weren't. At this point of my life, arguing with ignorance seemed to be more problem-some than helpful. The other dude who was involved in the almost fight came to me and said thanks. I noticed he would every so often drop by the church services and sit in.

In the middle of all this, I was still trying to focus on my character and my walk with Christ. I wanted to learn but realized some of the guys I was sitting down with at the picnic table were for some reason now, not all on the same page. Something happened! Being new in this walk, I was now seeing and experiencing for the first time, jealousy and envy amongst the Christian brothers. There was strife concerning who was right and who was wrong when it came to teaching the Word.

One guy stopped coming to the table and would just go on the yard and pray very loud as to bring attention to himself. I was still in my early stages and drinking milk but knew enough to know what he was doing wasn't right. It wasn't God, it was flesh. We are supposed to bring attention to God not us. This is not how we teach by example.

One of the guys pulled me to the side and said even though I was just coming into the knowledge of God, I would know more than the rest of the guys because I had better tools. I wasn't in a competition. Yes, I had been sent a real nice Dake Study Bible, but that meant nothing if I didn't understand what I was reading and lacked revelation of God's Word. The bible teaches to be humble and that is the way to approach His word. I wasn't trying to be the smartest or the most knowledgeable, I just wanted to learn more about God and get some understanding. I would bring my bible to our studies just to give all the guys an opportunity to research.

I was humbled to sit amongst guys who seemed to be a lot further along in the knowledge of God than I was. I was even grateful to have something to bring to the table. Some of the older crew stopped coming so we thinned out quite a bit. Myself and the remaining others would really push forward in the sharing of the gospel to different guys in the camp. We invited them out to just come and listen. Listening is the first requirement of learning. Even though the crew lessened, we still had some great learning experiences. Studying became fun and adventurous to me.

There's no other book ever in existence now or to come that will contain the truth like God's Word. The entire book is inspired by God and God breathed. His Word gives life and that alone draws me closer and excites my hunger for more. The Bible is a book about a King and His Kingdom. I, as a believer, am a part of God's Kingdom. I am a child of God and to know my entitlements I must, we must, read and study God's Word. We must learn His voice and listen.

His voice!!! That is what I needed to hear most at this point; because, there was so much tension on the camp. A handful of the inmates, for whatever reason, had issues with the Christians. Of course, I fell in that category. No one had said anything to me but I could feel the dislikes all around me. There were so many fake smiles but I tried to look past these things.

I knew the Lord was my protector and placed a hedge of protection around me without me even asking. He knew all that I didn't know.

I worked out daily on the yard and at times ran laps for cardio. One nice and sunny day I had just started a lap and had turned the first corner of the dirt track when one of the guys that had issues with me, who had also been in prison about ten years, yelled to me, "You'll never be like me no matter what you do." He was with a couple of the other guys that had issues as well. I was all alone on the track, and this time had to stop and respond, correctly. I yelled back at him so he and all his partners could hear me when I said, "I don't want to be like you, I just want to be a better me, no matter how long it takes."

This guy was two times my size without an ounce of body fat. I've had my battles in the street and wasn't afraid to fight anybody, but it seemed the Holy Spirit was once again showing me a different way to fight than I was accustomed. I would not have learned this new method of fighting unless I had these encounters. There is a process to being better and it was obvious I was in mine.

I must admit these encounters were uncomfortable and made my heart beat fast at times, yet they were necessary. This would not be my last encounter though.

The head cook, who originally spoke up for me when I had stopped a fight for going down, got an attitude with me for no reason one day. We were in the kitchen and he told me to do something because he was the cook and I was his prep cook. It didn't make sense to me what he was saying, so I responded as such, and he didn't like my response. He then jumped in my face and dared me to say another word.

He must have forgot in his moment of rage that as the prep cook I had a very large knife right beside me. It took everything in me not to stab him. All of what I would have learned up to this point would have gone right out the window. That would have shown no self-control at all.

What kind of example would I have been in that heated moment? Was I going to show that I couldn't withstand the pressure of the enemy attacks? Besides, I would have received new charges and going home would have been even further away from me. So once again I kept my mouth shut.

Later that night in the dorm he apologized to me and said much was on his mind and I did nothing to deserve his attitude. He too was about three times my size. I accepted his apology but was trying to figure out why I was having so many encounters.

To be honest, I look back and realize all my encounters were with guys two to three times my size but I still won without laying hands on them. I always prayed the Lord would walk with me everywhere I went in that place. I was new in Christ indeed and tried very hard not to allow my mind to revert to old ways of thinking. If I had, these different encounters could have gone much differently, and the story I'm telling now wouldn't be.

Being in Christ means to focus on being obedient to His voice and it is also learning to refrain from the old ways of doing things. That is a process!

The guy who had been mentoring me was in a dorm with this guy I did not know who was affiliated with a Muslim religion. These guys that I had problems with were also affiliated with the same religion. This guy was very quiet and always walked around in a polite manner. He would smile and speak and you always knew it was genuine. What I didn't know was that he had a lot of clout and when he spoke people listened. My mentor and brother in Christ was sharing the gospel with him. They were on very good terms with one another. Without my knowing until afterwards, my brother had a conversation with him about the problems I had been facing with these guys. This guy recognized my walk as being sincere and because I carried myself in such a way not trying to be big and bad, he spoke to someone regarding me and no one ever said another slick word to me. He was not a Christian but had much respect for my brother and much respect for my character as I was told.

That is what I call the Lord using anybody for His purpose. Even though this guy had all this pull, I don't think anyone really realized that my Lord, strong and mighty, ran that yard. Jesus called the shots! He allowed some things to happen for me to be strengthened and to grow in Him but what He did not allow was for me to be touched. The bible says in Deuteronomy 32:39, no one can deliver us from God's hand.

> **A thousand may fall at your side, and ten thousand at your right hand; But it shall not come near you.** *(Psalm 91:7)*

I know my God is a keeper and a protector. He is the Lord, my Banner Jehovah Nissi. In the Hebrew language Jehovah means Lord and Nissi means banner. This is to say the Lord, my exaltation. He elevates us to victory! He rises us above situations and goes before us in battle.

> **So shall they fear the name of the Lord from the west, And His glory from the rising of the sun; When the enemy comes in like a flood, The Spirit of the Lord will lift up a standard against him.** *(Isaiah 59:19)*

A guy, who I had shared the gospel with, came up to me on the weight pile and said, "I thought you were gone! I saw you at the gate leaving with your stuff yesterday morning. Only because I see you now, I know it wasn't you!" I said to myself, man that would have been kind of nice because this place was getting crazier by the minute.

The very next day, in the late evening, one of the main characters in that crazy crew got on a wild rampage. He was messing with people and causing problems in the dorm left and right. Something caused him to flip his lid. I wasn't afraid to fight him or anyone else; however, I knew I must try and keep peace. It was something about this night that I told myself if he came over to where I was I was going to stand my ground. This was right about the time our evening service was about to start. I did not want to miss service because I always looked forward to that time at the end of the day.

It didn't matter how hot it was in there. That was the least of my concerns and would not deter me from seeking His presence. While there, I remember praying for peace in my surroundings. Once service was over, I went back to the dorm and was expecting a peaceful night in my area. I did not care about what had happened earlier. I was going to mind my business and occupy my space.

Not long after getting back to the dorm, the correctional officer called my name and told me to pack my stuff because I was leaving in the morning. I was being transferred to another camp. I remember being overjoyed and saying Lord you move fast! I asked for peace but didn't realize it was coming with a move. I felt like I was getting out of prison. Guys in the dorm were like, you out? I was like, oh yeah!

I immediately thought about the guy from earlier at the weight pile who said he saw me leaving the day before. The Lord used him to see my exit and had him to tell me about it. The only part about this that bothered me was I didn't get a chance to say peace out to my brother, my mentor who helped me so much along the way at this camp. I will be forever grateful for his willingness to pour into me.

Since it was my last morning at camp, I was no longer working in the kitchen. So I was no longer serving the breakfast. The dude from South Carolina, that wanted to get in a fight at the food storage shed, served my meal. At that breakfast he said, "be safe."

I will never forget this experience here in Sanford. The enemy tried to pull me into fights, but the bible says, "No weapon formed against me shall prosper." This part of my testimony has come to an end and I'm off to my next destination. Time to experience peace!

# Faithful is the Lord

**God is faithful, by whom you were called into the fellowship of His son, Jesus Christ our Lord.** *(1 Corinthians 1:9)*

As I embark on this road trip, I have no clue where I'm going. I was told this kind of information cannot be revealed for security purposes so I'll just ride until I arrive.

As I look back at this camp I'm leaving behind, I've had trials and temptations; however, change took place in me just from being there. I can boldly say, how great is the faithfulness of the Lord!

**He who dwells in the secret place of the Most high shall abide under the shadow of the almighty.** *(Psalm 91:1)*

**His presence is our hiding place.** *(Psalm 31:20)*

**He keeps us protected from troubles and the plots of man.** *(Psalm 32:7)*

I could look back and say He has done all He said He would do.

**Commit everything you do to the Lord, Trust Him, and He will help you.** *(Psalm 37:5, New Living Translation)*

All He promised shall happen.

**Rest in the Lord and wait patiently for Him.** *(Psalm 37:7)*

I was much further than where I had started and have a long way to go. There was still so much for me to learn about trusting and having faith in God and I am willing to commit my life to doing so. I gravitated myself to so many things in the past that only brought me temporary satisfaction. It was about time I invest in something that wouldn't depreciate and would last forever. The salvation of the Lord has no end.

After all I had experienced, I was ready for a "ride out." I didn't know my physical destination but knew wherever I was going would be away from where I was. Knowing I was going somewhere better despite the circumstances was good to my soul. This bus ride was like breathing fresh air, releasing the past and receiving the new. My prayers were answered!

This trip was quite interesting because I was seeing some unfamiliar places. The longer we ride, I'm beginning to realize I've never been on some of these roads. Now I've traveled a lot of roads in my day but not these. We've been riding now for over two hours and it's got me a little confused. I know I'm not supposed to trust everything I hear on the yard but I did hear when you are close to getting out, you typically go closer to home and are released from there.

I was leaving Sanford and had lived in Raleigh so even though I had been gone for only a short minute I hadn't lost my sense of time and distance. Over a two-hour drive is not the travel time back to Raleigh. I would say an hour max just because we are on this bus.

Where in the world are we going? We seem to be far away from major highways and overpasses. I'm seeing all country roads, trees and a lot of fields. Why am I going further away from home and not closer? It didn't make sense to me.

I remember one of the guys at Sanford saying I was probably going to A New Directions which is a program for inmates who have DUI's and drug related charges. I knew nothing of what it was or where it was, I just wondered why the long travel time and still have not reached a destination.

Maybe we are going the back way. Yeah that's it! My mind began to wonder and had to grasp a hold of a scripture that would always bring me through since the beginning of this walk.

**Trust in the Lord with all your heart; do not depend on your own understanding.** *(Proverbs 3:5, New Living Translation)*

No, I didn't understand, but I couldn't let my mind get the best of me. I've come this far because He has brought me through and I know He won't leave me or forget about me. He has proven Himself to me many times over. I'll be alright. God is with me!

After driving four hours, we finally arrive to this building with a big cross on the outside. Honestly, this place didn't look like any prison I had previously seen. It had to be a prison because where else would the state be taking a bus full of inmates except to another camp.

We got off the bus and had to check in before getting assigned to our dorms. This place was so different. Outside I could see tables with umbrellas like those outside hotdog and burger joints. Prison, REALLY! Ok I'll take it.

The spirit of the guards was even different. They were calm and smiling and had been talking to us as if we were people and not prisoners.

We were in Spindale up in the mountains. The air was fresher and much cleaner. This camp was a lot smaller than where I'd been before and the setup was a lot more compact.

After getting inside the gate, the very first thing I saw were dogs. Now, I hadn't seen a dog in about four months so that was kind of cool. This camp allowed some of the inmates to work in dog training. They walked the dogs, fed the dogs and worked with them daily.

I stood in the yard and gazed at the mountains. I felt like Moses on the mountaintop at times being so close to God, yet so far away from the world.

It was ok at times while others were a little difficult. Even though I had not been incarcerated for years, I was still anxious for this experience to conclude.

Once again, the Holy Spirit was reminding me to trust God. I had to acknowledge Him in everything concerning me so He could direct my path. I prayed for peace and this is where He allowed me to come. There must be a reason and purpose for me being here.

Besides being behind the fence, this place almost seemed human, compared to the past camps. Not knowing anyone was always the adjustment for me but I quickly found out what I needed to know. My number one question, when are services being held in the chapel and how do I get involved. I was ready to go in and worship with new brothers.

My surroundings were a catapult into the arms of God. I loved being in His presence! It was the most comforting thing I've ever experienced. The love of God is better than any drug I've ever had, and I've had many. It's better than sex which I've had a lot of in my time. I'm not trying to glamorize sex and drugs in my life, but sex, money and drugs are what drove me, what motivated my life's movements. Recognizing the love of God existed in such magnitude was breath taking! I've never felt this sense of comfort until I gave my life to Jesus Christ as my Lord and Savior.

To know His Father is my Father and loves me like He loves His son Jesus is an amazing truth. He sent Jesus to the cross for all of us, just so we can experience life with the Father as Jesus does. He didn't want us left out or missing out on all the goodness of our daddy, so He took on all our sin and died for us. Our Father loves Jesus so much He didn't allow Him to stay dead, He rose Him up on the third day. The good thing for us is He took the keys of death from the devil so Satan was defeated before Jesus rose. He died and went straight to work just for us. Without Jesus, there is no life so anything before Him in my life was life in the negative.

I had the opportunity since I was new at the camp to go and see my counselor. After the counselor looked in the system my release date was reflecting only five to six more months from now so I guess I couldn't complain. I was just glad there was a date showing that was less than the original two years. Honestly six more months seemed like a lifetime but I didn't want to seem ungrateful to God.

I had homeboys who served a lot of years under their belts and what I was dealing with was considered peanuts to their bids. Even some of the guys I was locked up with had served over 10 years. One guy was in over 30 years already. This was new for me and to be real about it, if I had gotten busted for all the drugs I was moving prior to this stage in my life, I would have been convicted of football numbers as well. I thank God that I didn't get caught. He even then showed mercy on me because I always drove dirty!

For all those that want to attend the church services, we had to line up to be accounted for. This place has an actual church building which is why I saw that big cross on the outside when we first pulled up on the bus. It's beautiful inside and feels like it's not a part of the camp. You would think prison was not outside the church doors. It had those old pews like the old churches have but with a modern look on the inside. If it wasn't for all the green uniforms, I would have said I was not at prison at all.

Just like the other camps, outside ministries would come in and minister to us as well as lead praise and worship. It was awesome and would become where I spend as much time as possible outside the dorm and the weight pile.

My mentor from the last camp taught me a lot about technique and working out so I must continue. The weight pile is a lot smaller than Sanford and a lot busier, which means I must get in where I fit in. I linked up with this dude after working out on my own a few times and he started showing me some new routines. He was a real cool dude and I appreciated the lessons. We worked out a lot together and he even came to the chapel a few times here and there.

Everybody here kind of seems to be in their own world so I spent a lot of time alone at a picnic table reading my bible. Being in the mountains gives this prison a nice calming backdrop if you look at it from a different perspective. I tried to look positive at the mountains which are God's handiwork.

Where I could normally go out and take a run in Sanford on the track, Spindale is not setup for this type of activity. Sanford's track was isolated but here in Spindale the track ran in the center of the small camp that held about

236 inmates. Sanford was approximately 300. I could only walk here because the track was part sidewalk and was also right at the sergeant's office. I walked a lot here to keep my cardio up and to keep my mind clear. I am a thinker and my mind is always focusing on something. No matter where you are there are negative people around which is why I enjoyed walking and praying. This kept me separated from negativity.

I learned this camp is New Directions just as the guy told me before I left Sanford. There are classes you can take which are supposed to help introduce positive behavior skills and law-abiding behaviors. It is setup to teach all kinds of life skills and help those in attendance with self-improvement. It wasn't just about alcohol and drugs as I thought. As far as I can see there's nothing wrong with learning how to do better, it's just putting into effect what you've learned. A lot of the times the problem comes in the application. I wanted to apply better behaving skills.

I remember in one of the church services I heard a brother say, "Let God show His power in our problems." Why not? What do I have to lose, I mean honestly? When I wasn't screwing up and being a menace to society I was a real cool dude. I had to get to the real me and step out of all the lies that had engulfed me.

Not just me but everybody has a story. I had the privilege to minister to some guys and it's a real reward to see someone give their life to Christ and want better. I know God gets all the glory, it's just an honor to be a part of that moment when a man enters his next. It's like I've been through all I have just to come to this day and share with someone what I've learned and experienced in the Lord. It just feels good inside.

As bad as the concept of prison is, there are a lot of good people there. A lot of the guys in here have made mistakes that they would not repeat, because their eyes have been opened. However, the system is set such a way that some of them will never get out and be able to show the outside world they're different. Some have even had family to walk away even though they've truly been changed. Unfortunately, some bridges have been burned! That part of it is sad, even though we all have repercussions for our actions.

I'm so glad Jesus forgives us and whether we're in the system or not He loves us unconditionally and gives us another chance.

I had friends turn their back but my mother never did. No matter where I was she would come. She and her good friend would take that trip just to pay a visit. It's always good to get that kind of love and encouragement especially in the middle of your process of change. That form of love gives hope and direction.

Jesus doesn't hold anything against anyone. He wants us to repent of our sins and change our minds of how we look at Him and even change on how we look at ourselves. He wants to be our Lord and Savior. If we just give Him the chance, He always comes through and proves Himself. I have found this out personally!

For whatever reason, I heard my name being called on the intercom to report to the sergeant's office. Once I get there they ask me if I want to participate in a program that gives me early parole. What!!! Are you serious!!! Most definitely I want to participate, sign me up!

I had been here three weeks and things have already turned around. My Lord was showing His power in my problems just as the guy said at church. My situation was nothing to Him. It was big to me but little to Him.

I couldn't wait to get out of that office so I could do some sort of dance. I didn't know how to shout but today I was going to figure it out. So now I will be patient until my name gets called again.

I just focused on spending personal time with the Lord, working out and talking to some of the other guys. I've learned if you just be kind to people that alone shows a characteristic of Jesus Christ.

I would also just listen to people because at times they don't want an answer or a way to fix a problem, they just want a listening ear. We can get so wrapped up at trying to fix people's problems that we miss what is really needed. If you allow a person to speak sometimes they may begin to think about their issue and begin to verbalize what they think is needed to be done. They can begin to see where they may have gone wrong and what they can change. All they needed was an ear that doesn't interrupt. If you are invited to give an opinion then at that time you can tell what you hear the Lord saying.

I've learned a lot by just listening. I've even learned how not to approach a person with the message of Jesus Christ from listening to someone else say what is considered a turn off to them. I know everybody is different and receive differently so to come to everyone the same is not going to always produce the same results.

Even though I didn't like prison, I had to admit, I've met some real cool people since being here. The guy who had been training me, I wanted to show my appreciation so I would sometimes give him a soup (Ramen noodles) or the cookies he liked. In prison that kind of food is golden.

I had gone to the canteen to restock my locker on what I called Scooby snacks (taken from the Scooby-Doo cartoon), and my id would not allow me to buy anything. We had to use our prison id to purchase food from the canteen and for whatever reason it wasn't working at this time. I was really looking forward to a snack that evening as I had worked out hard that day. Even though they feed us three times a day I still wanted more.

The guy at the canteen told me I had to go to sergeant's office to find out why my card wasn't working. I get to the sergeant's office and find out I was being shipped out. Hallelujah!!! My card was disabled because I was about to leave. The Lord has done something amazing on my part and I can't help but remember the lyrics I've learned to the song while here at Spindale. The song goes a little like this, "I won't go back, I can't go back, to the way it used to be, before Your presence came and changed me."

Thank you, Jesus!

## A New Direction

    I am completely beyond myself right now. I am leaving these prison walls, exiting their gates. It is now the middle of October and I am departing Spindale, on my way back to Goldsboro, North Carolina to DART Cherry.

    DART stands for Drug Alcohol Rehabilitation Treatment Center and they have my name on a roster. DART Cherry is a chemical dependency treatment program that is made available for certain inmates depending on their charges and if they meet certain criteria. It is also made available for people coming off the streets in lieu of jail or prison time. The courts send probationers here also for rehab.

    For me to leave prison to come here gives me the opportunity for early parole. This means I must successfully complete a 90-day program and can afterwards go home. If I don't complete the program, I return to prison and finish my sentence.

    This facility is right down the street from the Neuse Prison Camp where I processed. At DART, I am not behind a fence with barbed wire. I could run away if I wanted but only a dummy would do such a thing this close to coming home. I am being trusted to follow through. We are even allowed to wear street clothes. No more prison greens for me.

    I have a four to five-hour ride ahead of me. Even though I'm still going to be under supervision, I'm finally leaving prison. After the long ride, I've arrived at my new temporary home. This is my last stop before transitioning back into society. For what I understand, there are a lot of rules very close to prison, just without the fence and the clothing. I'm down for the program and ready to get started in whatever it is I must do.

    Once again, I don't know anyone and only somewhat familiar with those who rode the prison bus with me. None of us were homeboys anyway but I know how to be sociable when needed. The building I'm in holds about a hundred men broken up into three separate groups. The groups are called Therapeutic Communities (TC). One TC was always at the beginning, another in the middle phase and the last one was at the end phase of the program.

These are broken up into the three-months program. When one TC leaves, another comes.

There is a correct way to do everything here and if it's not by the book, it's considered wrong. Doing things not by the book, at DART will get you in trouble. You are always being held accountable for your actions. It's almost stricter than prison and there is a huge price to pay for this freedom. By rules we must address each other as Mr. (last name). And of course, Mrs. or Ms. to any staff females we encountered.

My new group was recognized as TC-340. We are only allowed to talk in certain areas and certain times. Being silent was not that hard for me because I normally didn't want to speak unless necessary.

I was ready to roll out this process and put all of this behind me. I am very grateful for this opportunity and will take full advantage of it. I've broken so many rules in the past that I don't want to do anything that will jeopardize my freedom.

All of us are assigned to a counselor that basically writes up a plan based on our conditions and goes from there. The same study group at Spindale is the one that is used here called A New Direction. This group is a lot more intense then at Spindale. This place covers substance abuse, attitudes, character and it basically is setup to get you thinking about your actions and the consequences of those actions.

I know for me in my past I would disregard the consequences and perform any action I wanted. I just didn't count the cost. The only time I did count the cost was when I was being held accountable. Basically, after I got caught! Then only then would I consider my wrong doing. The problem with me was I would repeat this cycle.

Coming through this prison system really allowed me time to think. Back in Wake County jail my life flashed before my eyes and I saw my death. This prompted me to repent. I've had a history of inappropriate behaviors for so long that some things became a way of life.

In the past, I couldn't drive without having a drink or at least on my way to get one. I know it may sound crazy but to me driving sober was boring. My system always needed to be engaged. It seems as if I functioned better on the influence of something. This was all lies, but I had been convinced by the Father of Lies, this was me and would always be me. The devil is a liar! I would even drive intoxicated while I was carrying a lot of drugs. I just didn't care.

To begin looking at my thinking was a good thing.

**For as he thinks in his heart, so is he.** *(Proverbs 23:7)*

For so long I sold a lot of drugs and I used a lot of drugs. We become what we do often and I knew the negative patterns had to be uprooted out of me. So even though I received Christ as my Lord and Savior and had prayed for a new heart, I was not against looking in the mirror at me. Who was I? Who am I now? I am a child of God! I am a conqueror! I am a new man because of Jesus Christ. Who was I before? I was lost but thank God now I have been redeemed. I was healed and I was delivered but this place at DART Cherry was a chance for me to look at the old patterns and what triggers may have been playing a role.

I met my counselor and she basically asked my history of drug and alcohol use. She asked about the way I handled myself while under the influence. I always thought I handled myself pretty good. This lady seemed to be ok and was trying to help me all she could and I appreciated it. I told her a little about my past and she asked if I was craving and what I felt about alcohol and drugs now. I was never into telling everybody everything, just enough to see what you do with what I give you. I wasn't sure how she would respond but I gladly told her about my turnaround at Wake County jail and that I was now saved. I also told her I was healed! She was like well, ok, just don't be going around telling people I was healed by the Holy Ghost. Not sure what she knew about the Holy Ghost but it was obvious she was familiar. She let me be and I just said ok to her request.

I knew I had to comply to get through but I would not deny the power of the blood of Jesus for anyone's peace of mind. I would go back to prison for declaring the truth versus keeping my mouth shut to appease someone. Jesus heals and no one would change my thoughts or take that truth away from me.

This counselor just didn't know what I knew or did she? All I can do is be the example of what healing and deliverance looks like. Not to judge anyone for their beliefs or unbelief. My assignment even in here is to show new behavior and reflect Christ-like character.

The sleeping arrangements here were a lot more comfortable than the open dorms in prison. Here we have four- to six-man rooms. We are responsible for keeping not only our rooms cleaned but all the areas we have access to. This includes the shared bathrooms, TV rooms and all outside areas. Everywhere we went throughout our days, we had to keep clean and they had to be inspected. This reminded me of barrack inspections in the military but I can dig it.

My only issue is having to clean up after grown folk that don't like cleaning up behind themselves. All adults don't conduct themselves like adults in the bathrooms and that is the worst place to have to clean. Simple stuff like flushing toilets and wiping the seat seemed difficult for some. These are just a few of the things here that we are being held accountable to. If you were caught not doing something like wiping a seat or flushing the toilet, the person would not say anything and you would have a high chance of being ticketed without even knowing. These tickets were a system set-up to keep everyone aligned and responsible to each other.

Everybody knew at the end of the week to look at the posted list to see if they had been cited. The tricky part about that is even though you may have seen your name on the list, you wouldn't know who the responsible person was until we all attended what was called Encounters. This was the time at the end of each week you would have to go before counselors and SAW workers to have all tickets addressed. SAW stands for Substance Abuse Workers. They were the ones we directly reported to and who stayed with us every day and did night duty. They were in a similar role to a CO - Correctional Officer in prison or jail but not exactly. They didn't have uniforms; they wore street clothes like everybody else.

In Encounters, the person who wrote the ticket on you would have to look you in the face and tell you they wrote the ticket and why. We were being reminded about accountability for our actions. In response, you, as the recipient of the ticket, had to address how being written up made you feel. There was a punishment that came along with being ticketed such as writing an essay called a sanction or extra cleaning duties or even loss of TV or phone privilege. In the street, we called this snitching but here it was called making everyone responsible. I didn't like it honestly because it seemed you should be able to tell someone like a man face-to-face what your beef was.

You could only talk in certain areas and everyone was always watching for someone to ticket. There was no talking in the hallways, in the bathrooms or even when lined up to go somewhere as a group. It was like a ticket war and most assuredly all those wanting to write tickets on everybody else were the main ones getting tickets written up on them. Even in this you get what you give! The best way to not get ticketed was to check yourself and try very hard to follow the rules. If not, someone was going to bust you. Guaranteed!!!

We had the responsibility to meet certain schedules daily. We had classes, group meetings and different sessions on how to be better in life. We didn't have anyone holding our hands to be in a certain place at a certain time, we just had to be on time and line up as a group. Someone could go back and check on you but it would often cost you a ticket, especially if you were a slow mover and delayed the group.

When a class was close to graduating, we would have an opportunity to run for certain positions. Not everyone would have a position because they were limited in number. To get the job you had to be elected. These were not paid positions but gave huge responsibility.

I wasn't trying to do very much, I just had my mind set on doing my ninety days and going home. When time came up for election someone suggested I run for a position. At first, I wasn't in agreement and basically said, you go ahead and can have at it. But then I felt the Holy Spirit was leading me to do so. I was no longer in peace about not doing anything and just letting my time go by. I ended up running for a position called Department Head of Service Crew.

All the jobs listed are a part of what is called a structure board. To be on this board you had to be committed to the program and its rules. The structure board was what made the program work. It was like a government for all the residents. All of us as residents live in what is called a community. Even though we were all in the community not all were on the structure board. Your position on the structure board determined your level of authority. This environment was setup where ideas could be shared with the hopes of making things better for everyone.

As Department Head of Service Crew, the person is responsible for cleanliness of the complete building by providing all needed supplies to the cleaning crews. This position had no authority over the crew members but still had to ensure everything was cleaned properly and that all supplies were returned to their proper place. This position would also have to issue out cleaning supplies to all the resident's rooms. Rosters and weekly reports had to be kept and submitted that listed inspections and any difficulties experienced.

I wasn't sure how the election would go. I knew God had lead me to run for this position so I prayed that no matter what position I held that I would make the Lord proud.

If I didn't win, I was ok with that. I, more than anything else, wanted to spend time studying the Word. We had permission during our off time to utilize the classrooms we used for our sessions. I would often go to a classroom just to study in peace and quiet. I knew staying in the Word was now a part of my new lifestyle. It wasn't a jail house religion or a way to make prison time go by. This was my life! The Word was proven to be effective and I wanted in, all the way in. My relationship with my heavenly Father through Jesus Christ was the most important thing to me over anything else. If I got the job, cool, but if not, cool.

We did not have a weight pile here because it wasn't prison so I had to utilize everything I had learned in working my body with just my body. Since

I could go outside, I would do a lot of push-up regiments and all kinds of calisthenics workouts. I tried to spend my time here wisely and stay off anyone's radar so I really didn't know how I would be viewed in the election.

All 90 plus residents had to vote and it was to my surprise close to a landslide in my favor. All I could do was thank the Lord! Someone else had also run for the same position and received only a handful of votes.

This position was on the same lines of how you would run a business so to speak. I had to supply everyone with supplies and be accountable for where everything was. This utility closet was a mess and I had a lot to distribute out. It was hard to tell what was out and who had turned their supplies back in by the current operation setup. I had to do something different to make this thing work successfully. The Holy Spirit downloaded an idea to me where I made spaces for each room and each area to be cleaned. This new system would allow me to see what room or area had cleaning supplies checked out.

I got with a few of the residents and asked for assistance and we put this new system into action. The staff was so impressed that I came up with this new system because it saved money that was being spent on ordering unnecessary supplies. We always knew what needed to be ordered ahead of time and not at the last minute. This new system became effective immediately!!! I also received a certificate award recognizing my workmanship. Even those who helped me received certificates as well.

This was an amazing opportunity that required a lot of work and even supervision on my part. This position was tapping into not only the business sense of me but the leader in me. This position would prepare me for more in the future but I didn't really see it all at that time.

What I enjoyed more than this was sitting down and studying my bible. If I could do this the majority of my day with no interruptions, I would. Every day I would use my downtime to study as much as possible. I would go off to an area where there would be little disturbances but it seemed I would start alone but finish with some company. Guys would come in and ask for prayer or just be curious as to what I was doing.

Everybody here, just like me, had an issue or two or three with which they were dealing. If they wanted to talk, I would talk. I would do my best to point people back to Jesus because He was who helped me.

I went from just me in the classroom studying to me plus five and sometimes more. I never initiated a bible study; it just happened. I would do the same thing every night which was show up. Others would begin to do the same. They would just show up!

I often questioned myself and would ask God if I had enough to give the hungry. The Holy Spirit would always remind me, it wasn't me it was Him and He was using me. It's hard sometimes to keep your eyes off you, when you know you, and you're the one being used. It is a learning process to get out of the mindset of not being worthy or capable of doing the work of the Lord. I had to often remind myself I was forgiven of my sins.

I found myself looking at the old me when it was the new me standing there. I came to quickly realize others will see the new us before we do. I was discovering myself in God as I would minister to others.

Most times, I was nervous, because I didn't know if I would be asked a question I couldn't find an answer to or even know what to say. Trust me I'm not an expert! I just know what was done for me and I was willing to give just that. I am thankful to God because as I was discovering me, I was also discovering the power of the Holy Spirit. The Holy Spirit is responsible for bringing things to our remembrance and giving creative ways to answer questions that people can understand. Simple ways! Everything doesn't have to be deep just clear and relatable.

One young man, an Irishman, would always come in and ask me questions about God. He was a real laidback dude and felt his life needed a turnaround. I offered Jesus! I knew Jesus was the ultimate turnaround. Change is good but the type of change is what's most important. It's what counts! He like myself in the past said he would think about it but wouldn't jump to making a rash decision. It was all good, because I knew my Heavenly Father was pulling on his heart. He just kept on coming back. Keep em' coming Lord and I'll keep speaking Your truth! It got so good to him that he began to ask me in the early parts of the day if we were having bible study that evening. My answer was always yes! Even if I was tired, because some days I would be, yet, I would still show up.

Just dealing with my own stuff at times would wear me down; nevertheless, I had to keep persevering. Having bible study helped pull me out of my slump and for the others as well.

The Word of God gives hope and builds faith. It also builds a level of trusting in God even when we can't naturally see what we are praying for. We come to know His Word as being truth and it energizes the prayers as I know it can and will be done in the name of Jesus.

My number one priority was being closer to my Lord and Savior Jesus Christ. I wanted to make Him proud and to never regret dying on the cross for me. What He did for me and everyone else was because of His great love for all people! His love is agape, meaning unconditional. No matter what we do or don't do, He still loves us. He gave His life for all those who would believe on Him. And I believe!!!

My Irish brother came to me one day and said, "I did it!!" He was so excited and I was like, "Did what?" He said, "I said the prayer!!!" I was completely blown away and excited that he had said the sinner's prayer! This was worth rejoicing over and made my day. If I was brought here just for him then mission accomplished. To God be all the glory. He didn't say anything scripted because I didn't give him anything scripted to say. I just guided from the Word.

My own experience is to just admit you are a sinner and ask Jesus to come into your heart to save you. Believe He died and rose and that is salvation. The rest begins from there. I was a vessel being used to lead him to Christ and he accepted. I am so honored to be instrumental in people's lives being changed by God. As He was changing them, He was changing me.

My trust in God was still increasing! I love Jesus and want the whole world to know it. "Jesus loves me this I know, for the bible tells me so" and He shows me so! I don't just read it; I live it and experience it. Every day I open my eyes, I experience the love of the Father through Jesus Christ!

Even though if I had my choice, I would have preferred to be home, but being at DART was not all that bad. There was purpose in me being here and it wasn't all just for me either.

There were some real cool folks that were a part of the SAW team. They had to work shifts and to be present throughout the day. They also had to be present throughout the night as well. There were males and females in these positions and they were all good people. They also each seemed to have their own personal relationship with the Lord.

One worker brought in one of his own personal books for me to read. The book was by Bishop T. D. Jakes called "Speaks to Men." It was a three-in-one book that was so amazingly powerful and spoke volumes to me as a new Christian man. "Speaks to Men" was one of the three books in one and the other two were "Loose that Man and Let Him Go" as well as "So You Call Yourself a Man." This book spoke to the man trapped inside the little boy in me. I had to grow up and change my mental clothes. At times I was mentally dressed as a child but standing in a grown man's body. For me to be an effective man of God, the old man had to go away. There is no way we can move forward still being strapped to the old being. It's too much baggage, too much weight. It will cause a zealous person to become weary easily. I didn't want to become that person. We had to die daily to our old selves because the old man will on occasions try and poke his head out. It is very important to embrace the Holy Spirit. We need the Holy Spirit like we need air to breathe. We cannot make it in this walk without being in partnership with the Holy Spirit.

I was so, very honored to have crossed paths with a lot of the workers. They all seemed to be lead, to share with me and give me reminders or encouraging words. I believe the Lord used them to keep me reminded that He had me covered. One of the female workers wrote a scripture on a card and said the Holy Spirit told her to give it to me.

**For the Lord God is a sun and shield: the Lord will give grace and glory: no good thing will he withhold from them that walk uprightly.** (*Psalm 84:11, King James Version*)

What a promise! He just keeps His Word and not like people who fail us at times. I love the way He operates as His Word comforts the soul. He is always the same. No matter what period of my life God has always been God. I was just at one time too blind to see Him.

That same worker said the Lord told her to tell me, "that what I was doing there was only preparation because on the outside I would lead men." I didn't know in what capacity this would be, I was just humbled that the Lord saw me fit to be a leader on His team. People seemed to look out for me and the favor I was shown was beyond words.

**Bless the Lord, O my soul, and forget not all His benefits.**
*(Psalm 103:2, King James Version)*

How can I not praise the God who takes great care of me? Thank You, Lord for sending people my way to bless me, Your son. You Lord are the greatest!!!

# A Road to Remember

It's amazing what you can learn if you open yourself up to change and allow the process to happen. DART was not all focused on substance abuse and behaviors; it was also tapping into other ways we are able to succeed in life. We learned about business management and preparing for the job market. DART was connected to Wayne Community College so we took college courses that would award certificates of completion if we of course completed them.

I had the opportunity to write a business plan along with a few other guys as well as design by hand a business scale model. This was real cool because it allowed me to take what was in my head and bring it to life. Sometimes being so preoccupied with life we never take the time to invest in our dreams. This gave me the opportunity to see what I thought.

I also had a hands-on refresher course on how to work with others because in a team effort everyone's thoughts must be shared and acknowledged to be a successful team. Collectively we succeeded in preparing a model commercial fishing boat along with the business plan for the company.

We had an awesome instructor who you could tell genuinely cared about us. She even taught us about proclamations. These are to announce who we are and where we're going. It's very difficult to sell someone on you or your product if you don't believe in it yourself. These proclamations or decrees and declarations teach us how to command our day and speak who we may not see in the mirror into existence.

I've learned to daily speak into the atmosphere who God says that I am. Speak it so much until I believe it and then speak it some more. Once I believe it, I'll become it and others will see it and want it for themselves as well. We become effective by being the example.

It all starts with the Word of God and our faith in what it says. To be convincing to others of what we believe depends on us.

I AM THE LENDER AND NOT THE BORROWER

I AM THE HEAD AND NOT THE TAIL

I AM ABOVE AND NOT BENEATH

I AM A CONQUEROR

I AM VICTORIOUS

I WAS CALLED BY GOD AND AM WORTHY BECAUSE OF THE BLOOD SHED BY JESUS CHRIST

I AM HEALED

I AM DELIVERED

I AM SAVED

**Furthermore, because we are united with Christ, we have received an inheritance from God, for He chose us in advance, and He makes everything work out according to His plan.** *(Ephesians 1:11, New Living Translation)*

**And having chosen them, He called them to come to Him. And having called them, He gave them right standing with Himself. And having given them right standing, He gave them His glory.** *(Romans 8:30, New Living Translation)*

I have now been here a little over a month and it seems as if there was always something going on in the dorms we resided in. The current Senior Coordinator has been caught up in a minor scandal but major enough for him to possibly lose his position.

The Senior Coordinator was the highest position a resident could have on the structure board. The position would be considered the most respected member of the community. You would be expected to be an extremely positive role model with character that others should want to follow. The Senior Coordinator is the overseer of the entire house. He relates directly to staff and any information received by the Senior Coordinator comes directly from staff. He only relays information to two other TOP positions on the structure board and those two are to ensure the rest of the community is aware of all pertinent information.

The current Senior Coordinator was in the senior class to graduate next. He was in third phase. I along with my group was now in second phase. The Senior Coordinator had gotten in trouble and his position of function was on the line. This is not a position I would have considered for myself. Not a position I would have even pursued. For some reason, someone thought if he lost his position, I should be nominated as next Senior Coordinator.

This was not an easy one to walk in. People are already out to catch you off guard and eager to get you written up. To be a Senior Coordinator, you must know that people are purposefully gunning to knock you off. This is what happened to the current one. He was caught doing something that did not add up and he paid for it in a big way. The staff decided this position could not be vacant and a new Senior Coordinator had to be elected by the community.

I was even humbled that someone thought enough of me to be qualified for such a position. I realize more and more, I don't qualify me but the blood of Jesus did that. In any arena when I don't think I'm eligible, my Lord says otherwise because His blood was not shed in vain and not to be made light of. I prayed about it and decided to go ahead and run for this position. It was now left up to the community to vote.

One of my roommates, who like myself was a former Marine and a very good guy, also ran for Senior Coordinator. If he would have won the election, I would have been ok and not mad at all.

The only problem though, there was a major disadvantage for those running against me that they may not have known about. I had favor with God and man according to Proverbs 3:4. I had already won before the final vote was even counted.

After the announcement, Dimitri Rayner, in the middle phase, was now the new Senior Coordinator!

The Lord was still showing Himself to me every step of the way. With God, all things are possible no matter what it looks like or how "upside down" things may seem. The Lord thought more of me than I thought of myself. He took steps for me that I wouldn't have done on my own. He was teaching me how to lead by following Him. The bible says many are called but only a few are chosen. I'm starting to see I was chosen to be a recipient of all that the Lord has. This didn't mean I was just to get material stuff but I was receiving spiritual insight and revelation of who God is. I was also to be a giver of all I had received. I was to share the goodness, share the gospel, share the love, and to share the character of the Lord with others. I had to remember the spotlight was now all the way on me, and so what did I want them to see? I wanted them to see Him so the spotlight would be on Him and not on me. I was being watched by the staff and the residents. More than ever I wanted all to know Jesus was the reason for my season.

I was also excited because one of the guys who helped me implement the new cleaning supply system was elected in my old position as new Department Head of Service Crew. He wasn't even a believer but he increased when I increased just because he was connected to me. All of this happened because I was connected to God. God changed the situation not just for me but even for those around me.

In this new position, although I had more duties to perform, I was still able to continue my nightly bible studies. At this point I had a real cool group of brothers that were all on the same page. We would get together and learn from each other. I love to hear others breakdown scripture and give it life to the listener.

There was this one guy who I'll never forget. He was an atheist. He did not believe in God and creation was unexplainable for him. He and I were cordial and I knew the Father was pulling on him. He would sometimes come to bible study and ask a lot of questions even in his unbelief. This was tough at times because I always wanted to show people the scriptures and not just take my word for it. I shared with him about creation from the book of Genesis. I know God was with me and His Holy Spirit was guiding me all along. The atheist said if you put water in a bottle and seal it up, microorganisms would form so how did God create that form of life? I began to tell him how God created the bottle holding the water and He also created the water and the microorganisms that formed in the water. My answer was not complex, nor was it deep or even scientific. It was Word and that alone is truth!

> **For by Him all things were created that are in heaven and that are on earth, visible and invisible, whether thrones or dominions or principalities or powers. All things were created through Him and for Him.** *(Colossians 1:16)*

I didn't have to argue with him about creation or our difference of beliefs because that was not what I was called to do. I was called to give the Word and God would do the rest.

Not too much longer after this conversation, days passed by, this gentleman asked me to pray with him to be saved. All the times I've prayed with someone was meaningful but this was by far the most. An atheist, wanting to be converted to a believer, a follower of Jesus Christ, how amazing is that! All glory be to God! Jesus Christ is the Most High! By no other name than the name of Jesus can anyone be saved!

> **In the beginning was the Word, and the Word was with God, and the Word was God. He was in the beginning with God. All things were made through Him, and without Him nothing was made that was made. In Him was life, and the life was the light of men.**
> *(John 1:1-4, Revised Standard Version)*

The truth is none of us know the day nor the hour of His return so it's very important that we don't beat anyone over the head with the bible. We are to share the love of Jesus Christ and His truth and allow His Word to do the work.

I never had a lot of face-to-face conflict as Senior Coordinator but on one morning I did. We were lined up as a group to go to our first class of the day and one of the guys was talking in line. We weren't supposed to talk in line per the house rules so now we're held up because of having to wait for him to stop talking. When one does wrong sometimes others suffer. I signaled to him to be quiet and he then got real loud with me and by this time I had enough of his mouth! I Let him know he could get the fight he was asking for!

I knew I was wrong in how I responded. I was much bigger than that but he caught me on the wrong day and I was ready. By me being ready to fight at that moment also meant I was willing to give up all I had worked so hard to accomplish and that would have sent me back to prison. DART had a no fight policy and it would have immediately sent me back.

A couple of the guys I worked close with looked at me and said it's not worth it. They were right and I knew it. I then backed down and let it go. I expected to get tickets thrown at me from everywhere but I didn't. The guy I was about to fight was about to be ticketed for talking but not by me. I try to display Christ-like character in front of whomever I come in contact, especially non-believers. I knew conflict at times would be tough to handle especially in a setting like this but it was possible.

At the end of that day we had what was called a community meeting. This was held every Friday to begin our weekends. This is the time where staff as well as the Senior Coordinator and the other structure board members could address the entire community at one time. This is also the time where those who received a certain kind of sanction such as an apology or addressing their situation due to being ticketed would do it publicly.

A sanction is basically a penalty for disobeying a rule or law. You would have to say what you did, why you did it and what you have learned since you did it. We had to realize how those actions affect not just ourselves but others as well. We must address what our future direction would be going forward in similar conflicts. It was a way to see the wrong we committed and how those actions reap a harvest.

Even though I didn't get ticketed for my actions of response, I sanctioned myself and read it aloud to the community. This is how it reads as follows:

### *My Self Sanction*

I want to apologize for my actions this morning between myself and another party, which started as an argument but almost led to a physical altercation. This is not the stance I take as Senior Coordinator or as a man of God. I hope none of you have lost faith in me as your Senior Coordinator. My future direction is to think before I act in any situation. I have the tools and knowledge to get me through any situation, but these will do me no good unless I apply them. I will use all I learned up to this point to be level-headed and to make wise decisions. I am very blessed to be able to stand here and give this apology because a bad split decision could have taken me backwards when I'm supposed to be moving forwards. I have personally come too far mentally, physically, and spiritually to turn around now. I refuse to go back and I won't! We must all remember the tests will come and we must be prepared, and have a strong root to keep us grounded. May we all walk in peace! Thank you for letting me share.

I never wanted to portray that I was above anyone no matter what position I held.

**For those who exalt themselves will be humbled, and those who humble themselves will be exalted.**
*(Matthew 23:12, New International Version)*

The sanction seemed to be well received as it was given genuinely. I know I must work on this area of my life. It was a teachable moment and I know the Holy Spirit wanted me to see these weak areas so He can guide me into being better and strengthened in Him. This is necessary in all aspects of our lives because a negative or an inappropriate response can throw a brick in our progress if we allow it. This was a way of repentance and a decree that I shall do better because I am better.

Not too much longer after this, the senior class TC337 was graduating.

At a normal graduation, the Senior Coordinator would be a part of the senior class but as we know I was the Senior Coordinator from the middle class because the previous one lost his position prior to graduating. My responsibility on graduation day was to give a speech to encourage the graduating class as they're on their way and should be ready to take on the world.

I was told not to preach but be encouraging. I didn't know how to preach, I just knew no matter what all thanks should go to God. It didn't matter who you were because the good Lord watched over all of us, the saved and the unsaved. He was there with us and I was going to thank Him even if it was on someone else's behalf. I would just be subtle!

### *Inspirational Speech to TC337*

Good Morning DART Cherry staff, Wayne Community College Instructors and all D-building residents.

Today is a joyous occasion for everyone in TC337. Today is the day that you can all say IT IS WELL.

You have just proved many people wrong; some may have said all you can accomplish is being a failure and a loser. WOW, weren't they wrong.

You have just completed a ninety-day treatment program that some wouldn't even dare because of pride and fear. You've received GEDS, written resumes and business plans. You've even built by hand business models to show visualization of your dreams and hearts desires. You've proved them wrong! You've proved them all wrong! Most importantly you've proved yourself wrong! So yes, IT IS WELL.

Those lonely nights have all passed away. Those tears of fear that you can't be all you've dreamed, they too have passed away. But what you do have is hope. You now have a sense of determination that no one can take from you. That feeling of power, that feeling you have inside of you right now, the one that says I feel good and I look good, and when I get home, I'll be the one who stands strong. I'll be one who makes things happen, and not wait for things to happen nor just watch things happen! I am courage, I am strength, and I am love. These are the things you should be telling yourself.

Hold onto what you know to be right and true. Avoid down spiraling situations at all costs. Don't fall to negative persuasion but be a positive influence. if you fall...GET UP, wipe yourself off and try it again. Remember the one who loses is the one who gives up. The one who wins is the one who persevered.

    Congratulations TC337, IT'S OVER FOR YA. TO GOD BE THE GLORY. THANK YOU."

With these guys graduating this means the countdown for me is on for sure. Down to thirty days and I am ready to go home and start over. I knew I had to keep it tight. I had to be on my best behavior and watch my step. Can't screw up now; I'm too close to the exit door and off to real life.

  My focus is to pass these tests at the community college and press in more to God. My career readiness instructor brought books to the class and let us have our pick of the litter. I chose a lot of Christian books. I was really blessed to have crossed paths with my instructors. They were all different and played a necessary role in my life at that time. One was sweet and kind and another was tough and firm, but also fair. This was a reminder that life is not always going to be easy. Sometimes it's going to be tough. When we have God on our side we can get through those tough times. God is bigger and stronger than anything that we could ever face in life.

As this part of the journey ends, one of the final things we had to do was go to an outside AA meeting. This will be the first time I have been anywhere outside of the system since this journey began seven months ago. After getting to the meeting, I realized some of the people here seem to be doing ok and managing to stay sober while others had their daily struggles. I realize how important it is to pray for people because each one of us, have something we may be weak in but God can give us all the strength to overcome. I know with Him I can be victorious in this walk even though it won't always be easy. How do I know? He says I am victorious in Him and I have enough faith to believe it so.

> **But thanks be to God, who gives us the victory through our Lord Jesus Christ.** *(1 Corinthians 15:57)*
>
> **For whatever is born of God overcomes the world. And this is the victory that has overcome the world—our faith.** *(1 John 5:4)*

My thirty days are up and graduation day has finally arrived! I could run, jump and do backflips because the day has finally come. I have never looked forward to community time as bad as I am today. I not only graduate DART today, I am also receiving certificates of completion for New Direction, Career Readiness, and Employment Readiness all from Wayne Community College. I also received a Gold Certificate for Career Readiness from the State of North Carolina because I scored high in applied math, reading for information and locating information.

This is also sentimental because today I will give my last inspirational speech as Senior Coordinator. I was nervous because this process has been my reality for eight months. Even though I wasn't going home for another week, I wasn't sure what was going to happen. All I had left behind on the streets, I was now going to look in its face again and either embrace it or tell it to move out of my way.

Were my old habits still occupants in my house? I realized the house I was referring to was not a physical structure but it is my heart. I believed God to have evicted those habits based on my asking Him to move in. They both couldn't live in the same house.

I knew I had to encourage myself in the Word of God at home just as I have done on this short but long journey and be at peace in His covering!

**These things I have spoken to you, that in Me you may have peace. In the world you will have tribulation; but be of good cheer, I have overcome the world.** *(John 16:33)*

I had to remember God demonstrated His love for me that while I was a sinner, Jesus Christ died for me. No matter what I face, I am safe in His arms. I will face challenges but I am a winner.

**He who is in me is greater than he who is in the world.** *(1 John 4:4)*

**I can do all things through Christ who strengthens me.** *(Philippians 4:13)*

This is what the Word of God tells me and I believe it. I have lived it and He has proven Himself to me numerous times. Trusting Him is a must! I am not just telling you what I heard, but telling you what I have lived. God is so good all the time, and all the time God is good!

### *Final Inspirational Speech to TC340*

Good morning DART Cherry staff, all D-building residents and Wayne Community College instructors, with special gratitude to one instructor in particular. Your giving spirit and genuine concern for us will never be forgotten, thank you.

Well TC340, WE MADE IT! It's been a long time coming but we still made it. We've survived and we've conquered. We've shared laughs, frustrations, stories of disappointments; we've even had fallouts behind encounters. We've at times expressed anger toward others when we should have been mad at ourselves. The good thing is...we overcame. We've all learned how to turn negative feelings into positive experiences. Now, DART Cherry has been a golden opportunity for us all.

For myself, this may have been the last exit on the highway before having to spend a lot longer than the eight months that I've already had away from my three-year-old daughter. I now have another chance, we all do!

You see there will be people out there that are going to ask themselves, I wonder if he's the same as before he left? Does he still drink like a fish? I wonder if he still likes to get high! I wonder, I wonder, I wonder!

From this point on, we cannot just talk about it…we have to be about it. When people hear our name, they should be able to say Oh! If he said it, then it's true, because his word is bond!

Our families really need us. There are kids right now whose future depends on what we do as individuals. This means we can set the stage for our younger generation. A lot of kids and younger adults these days are lost and will follow in our footsteps to prison and places like DART Cherry if we don't get ourselves together. Our kids don't need us high, drunk and irresponsible. They need us alert and on top of our game.

REAL MEN AS POSITIVE LEADERS!

We've taken so much from people in the past, now it is time for us to give back. Let's handle business and be men. REAL MEN! There is always an ad that reads "WANTED." Men to be husbands to the husbandless, fathers to the fatherless, brothers to the brother-less and encouragers to the unencouraged. Let us all answer that call. Let's help change our communities for the better. We have a power within that strengthens us so we can overcome.

Make them proud 340 and let's change the world. TO GOD BE THE GLORY! THANK YOU.

I have assisted with the election for the new Senior Coordinator and the rest of the structure board. This part is finished.

> *You've survived the worst of time*
> *God was always on your side*
> *State your claim and write your name*
> *Walk into this wealthy place.*
>
> *I hear the spirit say that it's your time*
> *the wait is over*
> *The wait is over it's your time.*
>
> (Donald Lawrence, "Seasons")

# The Root

Even though I grew up in the hood, I was never a product of my environment as some often say. I was more of a product of my choices. "Straight outta" Armstrong Projects in Rocky Mount, North Carolina is where I'm from. Much respect to where I'm from and all I learned on my way, the good, the bad and the ugly. I am still on my path to my destiny and my past shall not be a hindrance but a catapult to the greater that has already been predestined for me.

I know people to this day that grew up on the same streets as me, who saw what I saw and lived in the same neighborhood I lived in, however they've never been to jail or prison. They also have never sold drugs or even used hard drugs.

They, also like me, were in a one parent home. I was raised by my mother and my grandmother contributed to much of my upbringing as well. I know it was tough for them at times and I'm sure I didn't make things any easier along the way. My mother was always working two and three jobs trying to make things work and to give me something better than the norm. While my mother moved out of the projects, I still always ended back there because while she was working I stayed with my grandmother most of the time who still lived in the projects.

I got real curious at things like smoking and drinking at an early age. I smoked my first cigarette and took my first drink at twelve years old. I also smoked my first joint at twelve. Sex for the first time was close to this same age as well.

Growing up I would at times wonder if my dad had been present, how would my life be different? I used to wonder what happened so bad between he and my mother that he would never come and check on me. I was born in Oakland, California and my mother and I left when I was two-years-old. I didn't see my dad again until I was twelve-years-old when I went to visit on a summer vacation. I haven't seen him since and that was 31 years ago. If he would have been there, I wondered, would I have made the same choices in my life!

My mother is very much into the Lord and when I was growing up she wanted me to share in the same beliefs as she did. She believed all that was in the bible and from what I could see she lived what she believed. Her faith proved she is a believer of the scripture that says if you train up a child in the way he should go, and when he is old he won't depart from it. She never gave up on me even though I didn't show much sign of converting to her same belief system. It wasn't that I didn't believe in God, I just wasn't ready to make the commitment that my mother had.

Growing up in the projects I saw a lot of opportunities to get money and that became my goal in life. I wanted what the older crowd had. They sold drugs, had money so of course had all the girls. The older guys seemed to get the girls that were in the same grade level as me because their lifestyle was much flashier. I knew for me to even compete in these streets, I had to be a hustler. Hustlers seemed to be the ones that got the kind of respect that I wanted. Money appeared to be what made the world go around and a lack of it made life boring and miserable.

I believed at the time, that if I was to hustle I would save my mother from having to give me money as she worked so hard to make ends meet. I just wanted to be independent and be successful at doing so. I grew up with a cousin who was more like my sister and a year younger than me. I tried to kick it with some of her friends but they all seemed to be more attracted to the hustlers.

One of our older cousins grew up right behind us and he always tried to keep me out of trouble. He was a football star and seemed to have it easy when it came to getting girls. He taught me a lot like an older brother would but what he didn't know was that I saw him more as a father figure. He looked out for me in the streets. Folks wouldn't even come at me sideways because of who my cousin was. I didn't have to do a lot of fighting because they knew my cousin would handle it. It wasn't that I didn't know how to, I just didn't have to that often.

I did though have my share of battles growing up as most project kids did. But those seemed to come more as I began to merge more into the street life. I was always considered real cool in the streets, even by the older dudes and of course some of the hustlers. My cousin was not that interested in the drug life and tried to shield me from that way of life. I'm sure he saw my growing interest. He'd often warn me about that type of crowd but I never listened. I always thought what I knew was good enough for me to flow the way I wanted.

One of the guys I began to hang out with made my dream come true when he fronted me my first gram of crack cocaine to sell. Fronted means I didn't pay up front for it but I was to pay a certain amount of what I earned from selling it. I thought that was the best day of my life especially when he taught me how to cut it up into smaller pieces to sell. I was around thirteen to fourteen years old.

What I didn't know was the crew I was hanging with was lacing joints with crack. I saw them crush pieces of crack and roll it up in the joint. I wasn't really into that but for the reason of not wanting to be lame I would hit the joint with them. They never forced it on me, it was always a choice. In my mind, I should do what my crew is doing even if I know better. The truth is I was good with just weed and drinks and to me that was cool enough all by itself but when it's being laced with crack that changes the ball game. My ignorance was not in the fact of it being laced but the affects that would later come. This new habit didn't last that long and me and this crew eventually parted ways. We remained cool with each other, just made separate moves.

I continued to deal drugs and was presented opportunities to deal more than what I had in the past. I made some mistakes and learned that money can ruin friendships.

I decided to take a chance and do something different in life so I enlisted in the Marine Corps while still in high school with the expectancy to leave for boot camp not long after graduating. At the time, I was seventeen years old.

Who would have thought 4-play "a la" House Party would be joining the Marine Corps. I got the nickname 4-play from the classic movie House Party featuring rap group KID N PLAY, because I drove a canary yellow Chevrolet Chevette, which was the identical car and color driven by Play in the movie. This car truly was a house party on wheels as it stayed smoked out behind those tinted windows of mine. During this time God was the furthest thing from my mind.

While in the military, I got married at the age of eighteen to a slightly older woman. I was still that hustler in a Marine uniform. I had the gold teeth and loved rocking gold jewelry. That was my thing! I never tried to be anybody else just wanted to be the coolest me I could be. I even brought hustling into our household.

While overseas I began selling alcohol that I bought on base for cheap to some Japanese people at double the cost. That is what you would call black marketing. I made a lot of illegal money while there until someone, a much higher-ranking Marine that I had much respect for, told me I was suspected of illegal activity because of my heavy shopping list at the on-base liquor store. I would sometimes go to the liquor store four times a day and even to different bases just to stock up. The more I brought, the more they bought. I made a lot of money doing this but knew my run had come to an end. There was a severe punishment for doing what I was doing if caught.

I craved living on the edge and would seem to run towards what I was taught to run from. After returning to the states I would later pick up a habit of doing a drug called acid because it was only detected by doing spinal taps.

I always seemed to connect with people living secret lifestyles and as they say birds of a feather flock together. I didn't seem like the guy who came out of a Christian home or one who gave their lives to Christ at a young age. Don't get me wrong, I had morals I just lived a lifestyle opposite of what I was taught.

Who knew that even then the good Lord was still watching over me! I had abandoned all my life lessons taught to me by my mother and grandmother yet God would always allow me to come close to the fire but give me a way of escape. He did it in Japan and would do it again my last year in service.

I was busted with dirty urine on a surprise urinalysis after returning from New Year's vacation my last year of service. I was found out to have been smoking weed. My rank was demoted from a Corporal (E-4) to a Lance Corporal (E-3). If I had not been demoted, I would have been promoted to Sergeant within a year or two. Honestly, I had the pills to take that would have showed my urine clean but I was too tired after the long drive back home from out of town and forgot to take them that morning. I didn't think at all and was not expecting this surprise urinalysis at all. It completely caught me off guard.

Even though I had this secret life, I still worked hard while in uniform. The problem is I was not being faithful to my position as a Marine when the uniform was off.

I learned who we claimed to be must be displayed not only in front of those that trust us but also when those aren't looking. What if there were no such things as secrets and all we did was displayed on our bodies and could not be covered up with our clothes. We would be literally naked and exposed not just for the outward appearance but also for the inward self because that is truly who we are. My inside man was embarrassed.

Those that I used to lead now looked at me differently because I was demoted to their equal rank. I was always cool with them and I never power tripped over anybody. That was not my thing, so when those that were once under my leadership were promoted, it was still love between us and no problems. I was proud of them for holding out and being outstanding Marines. I know there were some disappointments not only from them but also my superiors. At this point I was just ready to end my four-year term and disappear.

I was at the time also working on launching a rap career with an Independent Label in New York which I thought was going to be promising. I didn't want to get a dishonorable discharge because that negative mark goes with you forever. Even though I was looking at a new career I didn't want this stain on my record.

I had to get an attorney on base to represent me and it was somewhat open and shut until I denied smoking. They researched and thought it impossible to get THC in your system without smoking. I told them I drank something and believe I got it that way. After more research, it was determined marijuana can be brewed into tea and it may have been possible that was how I contacted it. I had to get a bunch of character witnesses and all my superiors stood on my behalf. I was found innocent and received my honorable discharge although I was not able to retrieve my rank as E-4, Corporal. I was told by the judge that as an NCO which means Non-Commissioned Officer, I should have known better and used better judgment in my decision making. My decision making is what got me into this mess.

It was within a week of me getting out and was advised to just walk away even though I could have reenlisted. I decided to walk. Even though I got what I wanted as far as discharge, I look back and say I lied to so many people that stood up for me. Even though I had high hopes and thought I was going to be a rap star, I still felt terrible about the way my Marine Corps term ended.

At this same time, my marriage was on the rocks, not because of the drug charge but because of my negligence to her and we eventually separated. I was so focused on making moves that for my family the time away caused a separation long before the legal separation.

I moved back to Rocky Mount and was still pursuing this rap career. My promised rap deal had soon fallen through and left me now having to find a job and look at other options. I did however find my first good job as a civilian although I screwed up some opportunities by failing drug tests due to my continued drug use.

I began hustling again but this time on a level I wasn't used to before. Someone I knew from the streets, a Jamaican, much older than me by close to twenty years, gave me an opportunity to get in the business with him. He asked what kind of money I wanted to make and if it was just enough to buy sneakers with or much more. I definitely wanted much more and had hopes to one day be on top in the drug business. I was only about twenty-two at the time and I jumped at the opportunity. We eventually rented a house together to make this business thing take off.

I started out getting about four pounds of weed, which eventually multiplied into forty to fifty pounds at a time. I began selling on average ten pounds of weed a week alone and increasing in cocaine distribution up to nine ounces which is a quarter kilo.

There were issues we had to face in dealing with this line of work because it was a shady business and jealous people all around. Friends were friends when they benefited but as soon as you cut them off, the shyster came out of them.

During this time, I began to sniff cocaine as I was told that it was a rich man's high. I was making money, had a lot of girls and this was supposed to put the icing on the cake of my life at the time. Man did it ever! It was okay at first until a dependency developed.

I started missing work which I was making at the time $32k a year at twenty-two years of age working on an IT help desk for a major company. My job interfered with my street life and I eventually quit my job because I saw more potential on the streets then going to work. A lot of times I overslept because sniffing cocaine will cause you not to hear the alarm clock especially when you lay down at the time you should be getting up. This happened often!

How blind I was at the time! I got deeper and deeper in the business and my drug habits got more and more serious as I moved up in the drug game.

One night my partner and I arrived home, just after getting haircuts and talking regarding arrangements we were making to open a clothing store that following week. Our out of town drug connections, who were also Jamaican, came by unannounced to our home. My partner stayed on the front deck while I went inside. I then came back out and we all had conversation for a while and it seemed all was ok but still, something seemed weird, them being there without notice.

One of them asked to see the gun I had used recently when I was shooting at someone due to a dispute. I was disrespected by someone I was close to at the time and had to go and do something about it. I jumped out in broad daylight and started firing a gun at a person that I cared about but in this business sometimes it is required or you will be second guessed in your future standing.

They acted as if they were really excited I had tried to kill somebody and wanted to see what gun I used. One of the guys asked me to leave to go to the store and get a blunt to roll up some weed, but my car dashboard lights for no apparent reason stopped working earlier that day and I didn't want to take the chance of driving because I didn't have a driver's license. I had previously lost it due to a DUI and never got everything rectified. I had a blunt I was keeping for personal use but rolled it up anyway.

I went to the linen closet and got the gun which was a 38 revolver Smith and Wesson. I handed it over to one of the guys only because my partner said it was ok. He was much wiser than me in this business so I trusted his judgment.

I walked away to another room in the house but after about five minutes I returned to the living room and asked for the gun back from the guy I handed it over to. However, the guy I had given it to passed it off to the guy that was with him. So now the second guy has tucked my gun into his pants. I got the gun back from him and then went into my room.

During the entire time, all of this was going on my partner never came into the house. I know he felt something was off but was going to let it all play out with the hopes they would have eventually left.

Moments later I turned around and looked up in my doorway and the one I had originally gave my gun to had followed me back to my room with a 45-caliber pistol drawn on me asking in a whispering voice for money and drugs. They took my gun off me as I was never able to get set in a good position to shoot or defend. I told them we had no drugs in the house although I was lying. While one was holding the gun on me the second guy taped my hands behind my back and even taped my ankles together. He also taped my mouth shut. I never suspected this would be the way I would go out but figured that life had caught up with me and I had made my choices which brought me here to this point in time.

That moment lying on the floor, I realized all the money in the world couldn't save me. I had money stashed away, I mean I wasn't rich nor had enough to retire but I had a little money but it would not have spared my life. Even if I had turned it all over It wouldn't have changed a thing.

All the girls I had been with could not help me. I had a girlfriend and a lot of ladies in my life but none of them at that moment could reverse what was happening. Their perfume nor their bodies that I adored could have gotten me out of this mess.

The drugs that I sold could not rise me above the situation at hand. The rich man high was not helping me right now. Where was the luxury of life in this moment?

This dude kept saying to me, he wasn't going to kill me but I didn't believe him. He turned my bedroom light down to very dim as they lay me on the floor face down. My partner who I really saw as my dad and the who looked out for me in this business had no idea what was going on in the back room while he was on the front deck.

They both then went outside with both guns and I heard some noise and then I heard what changed my life forever. I heard the shot. I was hoping to see my partner come running into my room but he didn't.

They killed my friend.

The guy who killed him then came back to my room and stood over me and tried to put the clip in the gun but the clip somehow expanded and would not fit into the gun.

When I saw this, I stood up and began pushing my shoulders on the window in my bedroom trying to force it open. I was trying to jump out! He was still not able to insert the clip in the gun and as I watched him repeatedly try I was able to jump out the window even though it felt more like I was tossed out. When I landed on the ground I had no tape on me.

I saw my friend dead on the front deck. He was shot one time behind the ear and died with his eyes open.

That night changed my life forever and it sent me into serious depression.

I didn't realize at the time God had spared my life. He stretched the gun clip so it wouldn't fit and even tossed me out the window. I can't imagine what the other guy saw as this was happening! He had killed before so this was not his first murder so I knew it wasn't like he was nervous. It was all God because that clip enlarged right before my eyes. Why did He want to spare me?

Instead of me running to God, I ran to drugs. I then started lacing blunts with crack and started sniffing more cocaine that I ever had. Cocaine became my breakfast, lunch and dinner. I didn't like going to sleep because I always had bad nights so I stayed high as much as possible.

In my head, I would replay over and over what happened and how I could have killed them and my friend could have still been alive. I always felt that it was my fault that I was not able to do more.

I took my remaining twenty pounds of weed and sold it all. I wanted out! All I wanted to do was get far away from people and medicate my pain. I didn't want to be around people that knew me. This once big-time drug dealer has now become a big-time drug user.

When I began to run out of drugs and money people started walking away from me. My girl at the time even left me and I know my drug habits had a lot to do with it. I was always high and making bad decisions. I was so alone even though I still had a few homies around me. I wanted to die and always blamed myself for not being a hero and somehow saving my friend. It hurt me more and more every day.

I moved to Atlanta to start my life all over again but I took me with me so it didn't work out like I had planned.

I met and dated this girl who was a journalist and she had started her own online entertainment magazine. She knew everybody in the music business and even those in politics. She introduced me to a few stars and celebrities and I was in a perfect position to launch a rap career as all the contacts I needed were at my reach through her.

I blew it though because I could never get serious about music due to the fact I stayed high all the time. I was always depressed and trying to relive life in my head before the murder of my friend.

I didn't know God had a different plan for me. In all my addictions, He was keeping me alive. I was unaware why God was allowing me to live but I wanted to change my life; I was just powerless.

I became really close with a family in Atlanta that I met when I had started my own carpet cleaning business due to being laid off from the 9/11 attacks. This family, they treated me as a son and I even learned some landscaping skills. They poured into me about God and showed me what love looks like. They showed me love without judging my condition and will always be in my heart. They don't know it but I call them my God parents because they were sent by God to watch over me as I was going through.

After a few years I moved back to Rocky Mount and tried again but that same guy always came with me no matter where I went. I eventually slowed down with lacing blunts but not until after I had lost so much. I lost respect for myself and it seemed as if I would never be the guy I once was. Even though I was once a drug dealer, I thought that was always the better me. Actually, that was not the better me.

I lost cars, residences and relationships all because of the bad choices I made.

After my friend's death, I was in depression for over ten years. I always wanted to have that someone in my life that would be a father figure or big brother type with no motives. I wanted my dad, my biological dad and he wasn't there. I was looking for relationship with others to take his place. It seemed that everyone that played that part somehow was taken away from me.

I do not blame my father for my life because I made my own choices. To be honest, I don't regret anything I've done because it made me the man I am today, the good stuff and the bad stuff. The only regret is I wish I had come to Christ sooner.

My mother did her best to raise me and she did an awesome job! I just chose to take what she gave me and sit it on a shelf for a while and live my life the way I chose to live it.

Rejection was very much real in my life. I felt rejected by my dad, by relationships I had with many different people. I always blamed myself for them leaving or not being there. I couldn't expect people to stay in bad environments, even though it seemed as if they knew how the environment was when they came into relationship with me. Why was I the one that people always walked away from?

It wasn't until the day of my last arrest that God was going to show me who I was and who I could be in Him. I began to feel the love of the Father and knew in Him was where I was supposed to be.

Some people left me because they couldn't be in my future. Others left because I wasn't supposed to be in their future. I knew a lot of good people wanting to have positive lives and I would have caused a conflict of interest so they had to go or rather I had to go.

I told lies and sold dreams to a lot of women and they would have been in a bad and hurtful place if I had stayed in their lives. I wasn't ready yet!

As far as my dad, I can't blame myself for that. I now have a relationship with him and we speak on the phone on a regular basis. I love my dad and no matter what he did or did not do that I felt he should have done, I forgive him. I also forgive myself! I appreciate what we have now and know that it only gets better as long as we're both willing to grow in relationship.

I learned the hard way that everything I was looking for in a person, God, my Heavenly Father was trying to be that in my life. I couldn't see it but He was trying to show me the ropes. I was blind at that time but now I can see He was always there throughout my life. He was there in near death experiences just as well as the good times. Every bad situation there was a moment of deliverance and now I can identify His grace and mercy being shown to me. I must do the same with God as with my dad which is, be willing to grow in relationship and it will only get better.

It's crazy how the entire time I was in prison I was being raised as an intercessor. An intercessor is someone who stands in the gap as being the one afflicted and prays for others. Enter in as if you are the one going through that situation and pray as if it was you and not them.

I have personal experience with rejection, bitterness, un-forgiveness and just different levels of life. I have not experienced everything in life but I have been through a lot. I learned the Love of the Father can bring us out of anything through Jesus Christ. No matter how big or how small, Jesus Christ can give us victory.

If you are in a place and not sure how you got there, do like I had to, and back trace your history. What you may turn up is some unresolved issues that have scorned you in your now. You may have people that you haven't forgiven or a situation that still needs to be addressed. These things can cause us to walk around in our adulthood with open wounds from childhood.

The good news is Jesus Christ is a healer and He is a finisher of His work. He will start something in you and will see it completed if you allow Him to lead you. You must surrender to Him and allow His love to guide your path in life. I know it may sound difficult but you can do it with help. I pray the help you need in no matter what area of your life is on the way to you right now in Jesus name. We cannot walk this out alone.

Getting involved with a good bible teaching church is a good place to start. The bible said we should assemble ourselves together and warn and encourage each other. Never let anyone tell you Church is not necessary. It is very much vital in our walk with Jesus Christ although church is not what saves us. It is the blood of Jesus that saves us and a personal relationship with Him is what you want over anything else.

Through all these years, even when I wasn't living for God, the Lord kept me and that remains to be true today even years later. As you learn to forgive yourself it will become easier to forgive others. We must learn to practice this if we want it in return. The Lord has given us numerous chances on top of chances and we should do the same for those we come in contact. Do unto others as you would have them do unto you.

I pray this has blessed you and there was something you could grab a hold of no matter where you are in life. God bless you and may the peace of God, the grace of God and the favor of God be your portion in Jesus name, AMEN!!!

# About the Author

Dimitri Rayner was born on July 13, 1975 in Oakland, CA. He was brought up in a single parent home by his mother, Minister Lillian Rayner. His grandmother, the late Allenia Bronson played a vital part in his upbringing. As a young child, he moved to Rocky Mount, NC where he remained until his graduation from Rocky Mount Senior High School in 1993. After graduating, he entered the United States Marine Corps where he served four years. Dimitri gave his life to Christ as a young child then rededicated his life in 2004, but it wasn't until 2011 that he began to understand who Christ was and what a true relationship with the Father really meant.

Dimitri now serves under the leadership of Apostle Dr. Shirley R. Brown at Destiny International Ministries Apostolic Training Center. Apostle Brown is not only his pastor but spiritual mother as well. She licensed him as a Minister of the Gospel in October 2013 and ordained him in the year of 2015. Dimitri's responsibilities include but are not limited to: the armor bearer to Apostle Brown; pastor at the Louisburg College Destiny Location alongside his wife; servant in the key leadership of Destiny and leader of the Men's Ministry.

Dimitri's favorite thing to do in life is to serve. He loves studying the word of God and being in His presence. He also loves spending time with his family, lifting weights, listening to and making music as well as being outdoors. Dimitri is the owner and operator of Groomers Outside, a landscaping business.

Dimitri is married to Valerie Rayner and together they have three daughters, Triniti, Ayanna and Adara. Dimitri is a man after God's own heart. Being a man of impact and prayer; a man of integrity; plus, a man of good character, he shows a powerful example of what prayer and faith in God can do. His favorite scripture can be found in Proverbs 3:5. *"Trust in the Lord with all thine heart and lean not to your own understanding."*